The Blazing Star

and

The Jewish Kabbalah

THE BLAZING STAR
AND
THE JEWISH KABBALAH

William Batchelder Greene

Foreword

by

R. A. Gilbert

IBIS PRESS
AN IMPRINT OF NICOLAS-HAYS, INC.
BERWICK, MAINE

Published in 2003 by Ibis Press
An Imprint of Nicolas-Hays, Inc.
P. O. Box 1126
Berwick, ME 03901-1126
www.nicolashays.com

Distributed by Red Wheel/Weiser LLC
Box 612
York Beach, ME 03901-0612
www.redwheelweiser.com

Cataloging-in-Publication data available
by request from the Library of Congress

TP

Printed in Canada

The paper used in this publication meets the minimum requirements of the American National Standard for Information
Sciences—Permanence of Paper for Printed Library Materials
Z39.48–1992 (R1997).

CONTENTS

FOREWORD

In its essence, the Kabbalah is a combination of a spiritualized cosmology and a strict ethical code, derived from an understanding of the true, inner meaning of the Torah, the five books of the Jewish Law. It was first codified as an oral tradition in the early centuries of the Christian era and has been preserved since the medieval period in such written texts as the *Sepher ha Zohar*. The Kabbalah is, however, more than a collection of ancient texts; it also encompasses the exalted spiritual experiences that arise when the dedicated student of the Torah's inner meaning attains that true understanding. But once Kabbalistic texts had been written down, knowledge of them spread beyond the Jewish community, and they were taken up by Christians eager to press them into the service of their own faith. With the coming of the Protestant Reformation, the once monolithic Christian faith divided, and with its division a host of sects offering strange visions of the nature and purpose of Christianity sprang into being. Some of them sought to justify their curious views by appealing to the authority of ancient, extra-biblical texts, including those of the Kabbalah.

Inevitably, the interpretation put upon these texts was unorthodox, but the majority of such sectarian readings still conformed to a standard pattern: humanity is in a fallen state and must be redeemed if it is to find its way back to God. Other approaches, even less orthodox and often eccentric (or original, to put it kindly), did not conform. The one trait they have in common is the stamp of the creative individual: they reflect all too clearly the mind and will of their creators.

Among the most striking of these unorthodox visions of the Kabbalah is that presented by William Batchelder Greene. It is grounded in his idiosyncratic approach to Christianity, which grew out of his private spiritual experiences. A sudden illumination that came to Greene during his military service in the second Seminole War led him from atheism to a form of deism that involved an intensely personal relationship with God. He had come to believe that "God is behind the complex of the laws of Nature—a self-acting, free, supreme, infinite Person, to whom all finite persons are responsible."[1] They are also, in their essence, one with God: for Greene, humanity has a common soul, and the soul of man is the soul of God. Despite this seeming pantheism, Greene maintained the mystical paradox of humanity being at once one with God and distinct from Him, and he advocated living our "Spiritual life in Christ by making him, his truth, his doctrine, our nourishment, even as we sustain our natural lives by partaking of natural food."[2] But our commonality of soul with the rest of humanity also entails responsibility: we will attain the divine state only by embracing progressive causes that will lead to social justice. Our template for this path is to be the Kabbalah and the magical theory that it contains. The Kabbalah, that is, as understood by Greene.

Understanding Greene's Kabbalistic system is not easy. He presents us with a man-centered Kabbalah—Adam Kadmon is "The Mighty God"—and gives an ingenious metaphysical analysis of the sephiroth: an analysis that reflects his personal, and highly idiosyncratic interpretation of New Testament theology. To compound these difficulties, Greene presents Old Testament proper names and symbols as having a socio-political meaning. He also relates Kabbalistic concepts to his own views on social issues and to his vision of an ideal society, and he creates an organic link between Kabbalistic and Masonic symbolism.

Thus, for Greene, the symbol of the Blazing Star does not have the meaning commonly given to it in his day. For most Masons, the Blazing Star was taken as being either an emblem of Divine Providence, or of the sun, "which enlightens the earth with its refulgent rays, dispensing its blessings to mankind at large, and giving light

---

[1] "William Batchelder Greene," in George Willis Cooke's "Historical and Biographical Introduction" to *The Dial* (Cleveland: Rowfant Club, 1902); reprint of the 1842 edition.

[2] Ibid. The statement was first printed in Greene, *Transcendentalism* (1849) but is omitted from the revised edition that was included with the original edition of *The Blazing Star*.

and life to all things here below."[3] Greene looked at it in a different way. The Blazing Star was the "Transfigured Image of Man"—
Adam Kadmon to all intent and purpose—with its form derived not
only from the interlacing of divine and human triangles, but also
from the uniting of the "working tools" of Masonry: the Square,
Compasses, Plumb-Rule, and Level. It is for Greene an emblem of
progress, and for this reason he chose it as the title of his book. *The
Blazing Star* is to be seen as a clarion call to the struggle for social
justice and the establishment of the religion of humanity. It embod-
ies the whole of Greene's peculiar understanding of the concealed
heart of the Torah.

How he came to develop these curious notions about the Kabbalah, and what led him to espouse his progressive ideals are questions best answered by considering his life. William Batchelder
Greene was born on April 4, 1819, in Haverhill, Massachusetts,
into a cultured, literary family. He was the son of Nathaniel
Greene, a prominent newspaper proprietor and editor, postmaster
of Boston, and a prolific author. William's education included two
years at West Point Military Academy, following which he saw service in Florida, during the second Seminole War, but resigned his
commission in 1841.

As a consequence of his religious experience in Florida, Greene
felt a call to the ministry, and began to study theology. In 1845,
after graduating from Harvard Divinity School, he was ordained in
the Baptist Church and served a congregation in Brookfield for six
years, after which he left the ministry and devoted his life to writing
and to active involvement in movements for social reform. This was
not a new venture for Greene, as he had been known as a contro-
versialist since 1842 when he first associated himself with the New
England Transcendentalists.

This loosely-knit group of theologians and literary figures, which
included Emerson, Thoreau, Margaret Fuller, and W. E. Channing,
came together in 1836 and exercised a significant influence on the

---

[3] Albert G. Mackey, *A Lexicon of Freemasonry*, 7th edition (1883), p. 37.

intellectual life of New England for some twenty-five years. Their ideas were derived in general from the philosophy of Immanuel Kant, who stated, in his *Critique of Practical Reason*, that "I call all knowledge *transcendental* which is concerned, not with objects, but with our mode of knowing objects so far as this is possible *a priori*." For the transcendentalists, our understanding of reality is dependent upon such *a priori*, or intuitive, knowledge rather than on objective experience. W. B. Greene became a part of their circle in 1842—the year in which his first published work, an essay titled "First Principles," appeared in *The Dial*, the quarterly magazine that was the organ of the Transcendentalist movement.

Besides their philosophy, the transcendentalists also had in common the tendency toward individualism. In Greene this trait was especially marked. He held independent views on the nature of Transcendentalism, as is clear from the pamphlet of that name which he published in 1849. Transcendentalism is there defined as "that form of philosophy which sinks God and Nature in man."[4] He saw it also less as a set of doctrines than as "a point of view," and his own viewpoint affirms "that the soul creates all things— man, the universe, all forms, all changes, and that this wonderful power is possessed by each individual soul."[5] This, however, is only a part of the larger picture, for "The man, therefore, who has attained to right knowledge is aware that there is no such thing as an individual soul. There is but one soul, which is the Over Soul, and this one soul is the animating principle of all bodies."[6] Such a belief fits well with the Unitarian form of Christianity that Greene had, by this time, espoused. His views are also set out in detail in his first book, *Remarks on the History of Science followed by an* A *Priori Autobiography* (Boston, 1849). It is an odd book, published anonymously, and consisting almost entirely of a reflective, spiritual-philosophical autobiography that tells virtually nothing of the author's outer life. What is clear from the contents, however, is that

---

[4] "New England Trancendentalism," in *The Blazing Star* (1872), p. 49.
[5] Ibid., p. 161.
[6] Ibid., p. 162.

Greene was certainly well-read in both philosophy and comparative religion, conversant with Jacob Boehme, and familiar with contemporary French writers, whether esotericists such as Fabre d'Olivet, or "religious" social philosophers such as Pierre Buchez and the Comte de Saint-Simon. There is, however, nothing in Greene's writings at this time to indicate that he knew anything at all about the Kabbalah.

This is not as surprising as it may appear at first sight. In 1849, nothing specific on the Kabbalah was available in print in English, nor would there be until Ginsburg published his seminal essay in 1865.[7] Not that Greene needed Kabbalistic texts at this time; he would not make use of them for another twenty years, after his first visit to Europe and the completion of his radical education.

Between 1853 and 1859 Greene lived in Paris and was heavily influenced by French progressive thought. His sympathy for the *communards* of 1871 is explicit, and follows naturally from his active support in America for mutual banking, true popular government, and the advancement of the working classes. And in France, Greene also advanced his knowledge of occultism. He entered Freemasonry and became a member of one of the Parisian lodges under the Grand Orient of France. Unlike its English and American counterparts, French Freemasonry did not forbid the discussion of religion or politics and many of its members held pronounced radical and anticlerical views. There was also a parallel strain of esoteric Masonry, and a combination of two such approaches evidently proved highly congenial to Greene. However, his introduction to the Kabbalah probably came from outside French Masonic circles. The most likely source was the writings of Eliphas Lévi, and it is tempting to speculate that Greene may have met Lévi during his time in Paris, but there is no evidence that such a meeting took

---

[7] Christian D. Ginsburg, *The Kabbalah: Its Doctrines, Development, and Literature: An Essay* (London, 1865). One earlier work which includes a chapter on the sephiroth was published in New York in 1859: a translation by Max Wolff of a French work of 1851, David Rosenberg's *Explication of an Engraving Called the Origin of the Rites and Worship of the Hebrews; together with Remarks on Creation.*

place. However, Lévi's most important occult work, *Dogme et Rituel de la Haute Magie*, the first volume of which contains much on the Kabbalah, was published in 1856 and Greene may have bought a copy at the time (although he credits a Masonic friend for bringing to his notice the illustrations that he reproduces in *The Blazing Star*). Greene may also have read the Kabbalistic articles that Lévi contributed to his own journal, *la Revue Philosophique et Religieuse*, during 1855, and possibly Adolphe Franck's *Le Kabbale, ou la philosophie religieuse des Hébreux*, which had appeared in 1843. Franck quotes extensively from the Zohar but his quotations do not match those given by Greene, who may thus be presumed to have turned to *Kabbala Denudata* (1677–1684), Knorr von Rosenroth's partial translation into Latin, for his Zoharic texts.

But whatever the source of his knowledge, Greene returned from France enthused by Kabbalistic speculation and eager to relate it to his own transcendentalist, social Christianity. His work was interrupted by the Civil War, in which he played an active part as colonel of the Fourteenth Massachusetts Volunteers, but he was able to publish one pamphlet, *Consciousness as Revealing the Existence of God, Man and Nature*, in 1864. Other pamphlets followed, on philosophy, mathematics, and social issues, but his creative energy was reserved for *The Blazing Star*. It received little notice on publication and virtually none in the Masonic press. Only one Masonic journal reviewed the book. In the *Freemasons' Monthly Magazine*,[8] published in Boston, Charles Moore, the editor, reported on it briefly but favorably. *The Blazing Star* was, he noted, "exceedingly well written and logically reasoned," and "perhaps one of the most remarkable and erudite little volumes" to come his way. It was, however, "too abstruse and metaphysical for the general reader"—an all-embracing term that included the average Freemason.

What is noticeable, yet hardly surprising, about Moore's notice is that he does not refer to Greene as a Freemason. In 1871, the Grand Orient of France was still recognized by the Grand Lodges in North America—recognition was withdrawn in 1878 when the

---

[8] Vol. 31, no. 8, June 1, 1872, pp. 254-255.

Grand Orient ceased to require its members to affirm a belief in God—and Greene would have been able to attend Masonic meetings in Boston and elsewhere had he so wished. That he did not, despite his friendship with C. L. Woodbury, a prominent Boston lawyer and Freemason, suggests that he found American Masonry uncongenial. Certainly he would have been appalled by the use of an inverted pentagram—which he describes as a "detestable sign"—as the emblem of the Order of the Eastern Star, and he was clearly unfamiliar with the recognized interpretations of other Angle-Saxon Masonic symbols. There can also be no doubt that his ignorance of Masonic niceties contributed to the book's failure to be taken up in Masonic circles—even those consisting of enthusiasts for occultism.

Nor was *The Blazing Star* seized upon by non-Masonic occultists, either at the time of publication or later. There is no reference to it in *Isis Unveiled*, and none in Theosophical, Rosicrucian, or Spiritualist periodicals, whether American or English. It is not mentioned in Isaac Myer's *Qabalah* (1888), nor in Mathers's *Kabbalah Unveiled* (1887); Westcott ignored the book and only A. E. Waite gave it any recognition. It should not be assumed that occultists, Freemasons, and others dismissed the book as worthless: a more likely explanation is that they were ignorant of it. Very few reviews had appeared, it was not held by most of the accessible institutional libraries, and it was absent from both the Westcott Hermetic Library and the Second Order Library of the Golden Dawn. Waite, however, had better opportunities than most of his contemporaries for finding obscure books through his association with the occult publisher and bookseller, George Redway.

Exactly when Waite read *The Blazing Star* is not known, but by 1899, when he wrote *The Doctrine and Literature of the Kabalah*,[9] he was familiar with the text and with Greene's unorthodox ideas. He cites the book three times when setting out the nature of the

---

[9] Owing to a fire at the printer's, Ballantyne, and the subsequent failure of Redway's publishing house, the book did not appear until 1902, when it was published by the Theosophical Publishing Society.

Kabbalah, especially to emphasize its theosophical rather than its magical nature, but without endorsing Greene's views,[10] Waite also emphasizes the obscurity of the book by referring to Greene as "an almost unknown writer." This suggests that English occultists, including Waite, had been utterly unaware that William Batchelder Greene had lived among them for the last five years of his life.

After the publication of *The Blazing Star*, Greene returned to his radical pursuits, but for reasons unknown he emigrated to England in 1873, remaining there until his death on May 30, 1878. He continued to write social and economic pamphlets in support of the working class, but he had no known involvement with Freemasonry or with any form of occultism. It is one of the great ironies of esoteric history that Greene should have remained in such obscurity, for the seaside town in which he died, Weston-super-Mare, was the center of a remarkable group of Masonic Rosicrucians that included F. G. Irwin, Benjamin Cox and, in the 1870s, William Wynn Westcott. Had these inspirers, creators, and supporters of the Hermetic Order of the Golden Dawn known that an enthusiastic and highly articulate esoteric scholar was living quietly in their midst, they would certainly have drawn him into their circle. If this had happened, then the Golden Dawn would have been influenced less by an imaginary German adept than by a real and living American Kabbalist.

R. A. Gilbert,
Bristol, September 2003

---

[10] *Doctrine and Literature of the Kabalah*, see pp. 22, 24-25, and 71. The quotations and footnotes are retained in *The Holy Kabbalah* (1929), pp. 33, 34, and 217.

THE BLAZING STAR

Some men—not all men—see always before them an ideal, a mental picture if you will, of what they ought to be, and are not. Whoso seeks to follow this ideal revealed to the mental vision, whoso seeks to attain to conformity with it will find it enlarge itself, and remove from him. He that follows it will improve his own moral character; but the ideal will remain always above him and before him, prompting him to new exertions. What is the natural conscience if it be not a condemnation of ourselves as we are, mean, pitiful, weak, and a comparison of ourselves with what we ought to be, wise, powerful, holy?

It is this Ideal of what we ought to be, and are not, that, is symbolically pictured in the Blazing Star.

The abject slave on an East-African rice plantation, brutal, ignorant, and a devil-worshipper, sees this Day-Star rising, in his heart, and straightway he becomes intellectually of age. For it is the soul, not the body, that attains to the age of discretion. They who see this Star, have attained to their majority: all other persons are minors. Before the rays of this Star, voudouism and devil-worship, whether in refined societies, or among barbarous peoples, vanish into night; for immersion into the rays of this Star, is the beginning of the baptism of repentance and penance for the remission of sin—and of the penalties of sin.

***

Whoso beholds this Star acquires FAITH. Faith is conviction born from the consciousness of aspiration. Faith is the active principle of intellectual progress.

The Blazing Star is the transfigured image of man—the Ideal that removes farther and farther, making always higher and higher claims, until, at the last, it becomes lost in infinity; and faith affirms that this same Blazing Star may be, *perhaps*, the shadowy, imperfect, and inadequate image of some unknown and invisible God.

Now, if it be true that God and man are in one image or likeness (and the affirmation that they are so is not implausible) then it is the duty of man to bring out into its full splendor that Divine Image which is latent, on one side, in the complexity of his own nature. This conclusion confirms itself.

You say you will never believe in God until the fact of his existence is proved to you! Then you will never believe in him at all; for, in the face of positive knowledge, faith is no longer possible. Faith affirms in the presence of the unknown. If science should ever demonstrate the existence of God (which it never can) faith would become lost in sight, and men would no longer believe, but know. The reason why science is intrinsically incompetent to either prove or disprove the existence of God, is simply this, that the subject matter transcends the reach of scientific instruments and processes. The dispute is, therefore, not between faith and science, but between faith and unbelief. Unbelief is a disease, not of the human understanding, but of the human will, and is susceptible of cure.

Saint Paul says, "We walk by faith, and not by sight"; again, "We see through a glass darkly"; and again, "We are saved by hope, but hope that is seen is not hope." Do what we will, we are under the necessity of walking, much more than half our time, not by sight, but by faith. The better half of our life upon the earth, and the happier half, is the part that is spent in advance of positive knowledge.

Science is constantly encroaching on the domains of faith, by showing that postulates of faith are demonstrably correct. But whenever any postulate of faith is proved, and thus becomes a truth of science, and no longer a truth of faith, faith immediately passes again to the front, with the affirmation of a new, and a higher, postulate. Faith keeps always well in advance of science.

Legitimate science never arrays itself in a hostile attitude against genuine faith. Science, it is true, often successfully refutes dogmas that are alleged to be of faith; but, in such cases, it is always found, upon due observation and inquiry, that the dogmas so refuted were born, not at all of faith, but of political or clerical ambition, or of fear, or of self-interest, or of the presumption of ignorance, or of some other human passion—or, perhaps, of sheer stupidity. Superstition, fanaticism and bigotry are signs and marks showing that the soul is not yet intellectually of age. They never result from convictions born of the consciousness of aspiration, and are, therefore, never of faith.

Faith does not say, Is there a God? It is doubt that says that. Faith says, Why should there not be a God? Absolute perfection is no natural obstacle to existence, but the contrary. Faith says, Figure to yourself, if you can, that there is no God! You cannot do it.

Faith is the affirmation respecting things unknown, that is implied in the practical recognition of known absurdity as such. Faith is reason denying absurdity in the face of the unknown.

An admissible definition of God must be in the form of a negative pregnant—an affirmation of God as that unknown Absolute and Infinite, which is the reason of the existence of the known finite and relative that we ourselves are.

Faith is from within; it is the outbreaking of human spontaneity; it is force of soul, grandeur of sentiment, magnanimity, generosity, courage. Its formulas are naturally unintelligible in their literal tenor; for, otherwise, they would represent that which is scientifically known, and would not be the mere provisional clothing of that which is not objectively given, but subjectively[1] projected from the inmost depth of the soul. Man, having an ideal before him of that which he ought to be, and is not, and acting as though he possessed the character he ought to have, but has not, comes, by the very virtue of his aspiration, to possess the character he imagines. Thus the world is leavened. Materialism, the spiritual death which is consequent upon the subordination of the subject to the object in thought, is the very soil from which faith springs; for every thing that stands by itself alone, makes way, through the necessity of the principle of contradictions, for its correlative opposite. Stoicism has always its birth in Sybaritic cities, and among over-civilized and effete peoples. Men learn, through faith,

---

[1] That is *subject* which calls itself Ego, *I*. That is *object* which the *I* contadistinguishes from itself, calling it *non-Ego*. That is *subjective* which belongs to the subject; and that *objective* which belongs to the object.

to do always the very thing they are afraid to do, and thus come to fear no longer. Unbelief naturally gives emptiness of heart; and emptiness of heart surprises itself with spontaneity of worship; and spontaneous worship gives the worshipper something of the high nature of that which is worshipped; and, in this way, unbelief transfigures itself, and loses itself in faith. Faith may always be acquired. Whoso is devoid of faith, and desires to have it, may acquire it by living for a few days (sometimes for a few hours only) as though he already possessed it. It is by practical, not theoretical, religion, that men transform their lives. By the practice of faith, man grows strong in faith. The moral coward becomes a moral hero as soon as he acquires faith. Weak women, among the early martyrs, learned by faith to face the wild beasts. When they were thrown to the lions, the lions trembled; for the women were more lion-like than the lions; and the lions knew it.

✳✳✳

Man has a threefold nature. He is, therefore, symbolically represented under the similitude of a triangle. Saint Paul says that man is body, soul, and spirit; and Saint Augustin says that he is will, understanding, memory. One philosopher says that man is intelligence, activity, and sensibility; another says that he is sensation, sentiment, cognition; and other philosophers give other formulas. But there exists no extant denial (at the least, none such exists to our knowledge) of the essential triplicity of man's nature.

✳✳✳

The Ideal is the invisible Sun which is always on the meridian of the soul. As the ever-revolving earth rises and sets upon the sun, which is steadfast, and not the sun on the earth, so the soul rises or sets on the Ideal; which is what it is whether man behold it or not, and is itself unaffected by man's attitude in respect to it, since it is the fixed centre, and the Day-Star of spiritual existences. It was for this reason that the temples were always opened in the ancient times, for purposes of initiation, at what was mystically called "high noon," although, in point of practical fact, that same "high noon" often occurred at the dead of night. This Day-Star was known in the temples as *Bel-samen,* the Lord of Heaven—as *Mithras* also, or as *Osiris,* or *Apollo,* or, more mystically, as *Abrasax,* and by a thousand other names. In the public worship, it was recognized as the visible sun; but in the esoteric work, after the avenues of the temples were duly guarded against cowans and eavesdroppers, as the Ideal-Man, and as the Star of souls.

✶✶✶

The five-rayed Blazing Star—the Pentacle—ABRAK—is the special star of the great Aryan (or Indo-Germanic, or Japhetic[2]) race. [The Shemite knows it not.] This Star —ABRAK—is a disguised image or likeness of man. The superior ray represents the head; the horizontal rays, the two arms; and the inferior rays, the two legs. This Star, being unsymmetrical, is capable of being turned upside down. It is our intention to explain, at some future time, the terrible meaning that is presented by the five-rayed Star, when its point is turned downward. Let it suffice to say, here, in passing, that this detestable sign (the inverted Star) execrated by the more intelligent adepts themselves in perverted mysteries, and excluded from their midnight orgies, is the head of the famous goat that plays so important a part in the ceremony of obscene initiations. The two ascending rays are the

---

[2] "These are *the generations* of Noah: Noah was a just man, *and perfect in his generations,* and Noah walked with the Elohim. And Noah begat three sons, *Shem, Ham,* and *Japhet.* "—*Gen.* vi. 9–10.

goat's horns, the horizontal rays are his two ears, and the descending ray is his beard.[3]

The Shemitic race, the equal of the Aryan, and in some respects its superior, knows not ABRAK: it sees not that inner light which the Aryan sees, and of which we have all along been speaking. But, instead, the Shemite hears inwardly—as the Aryan does not—mysterious and unspeakable words which it is not lawful for a man to utter. To the Shemite, conscience is not at all a comparison, as it is to the Aryan, of what man makes real in himself, with the ideal always before him of what he ought to so make real, but is, on the contrary, the actual voice of God speaking inwardly to the soul. The Aryan objectivizes all things. He forms conceptions tangible to the imagination; and what he is incompetent to clearly conceive, he discards as unreal. He naturally gives form and expression, through symbolic art, to his inward thought; and, until his thought is expressed in form, it is, to him, as though it existed not. To the Shemite, on the contrary, all visible symbols, whether discernible to the outward or to the inward eye, are worse than worthless. The poetry of the Aryans is objective and descriptive; that of the Shemites is sometimes didactic, sometimes lyrical, but never objective. The Shemite has no plastic and no pictorial art. The religion of the Aryan is that of the revealed Ideal; the religion of the Shemite is that of the revealed Word. The conscience is the essential religious faculty of man; and it is in the divergent natures of the Aryan and Shemitic consciences, that the root of the divergencies of the Aryan and Shemitic religions

---

[3] The human hand, with the thumb and fingers, is the five-rayed Star; but with the three larger fingers closed, and the thumb and little finger protruding (the common counter-charm to the evil-eye) it is that Star inverted, or the goat's head. The hand with the three larger fingers closed, is the negation of the ternary, and the affirmation of the antagonistic natural forces only. The thumb represents generative power, and the little finger denotes insinuating tact: the hand, therefore, that shows the thumb and little finger only, denotes passion united with address. The thumb is the synthesis of the whole hand. A morally strong man has always a strong thumb; and a weak man, a weak thumb. A long thumb denotes obstinacy. Blessings are conferred with two of the larger fingers, or with all three of them. The thumb and little finger are used in cursing.

is to be sought and found. The spirit of the Shemite continually groans and travails within itself, waiting for the utterance of unspoken words; and it revels in the consciousness of that which it knows to be at once real and inconceivable. When the great wind rent the mountains, and broke the rocks in pieces before Elijah (a Hebrew Shemite) the prophet could not see God in the wind. Neither could he see God in the earthquake that followed the wind, or in the fire that followed the earthquake. But, after the fire, there came "a still small voice"; and, when Elijah *heard that,* be wrapped his face in his mantle, and went to the mouth of the cave, and stood up before Jehovah. It was the "word" of the Lord that came to the greater Hebrew prophets; and it was only by prophets of lesser note that "visions " were seen in deep sleep, when they were upon their beds. The greater prophets *heard* in ecstatic trances; but they seldom *saw* clairvoyantly. It would seem that God is nearer to the Shemite than he is to the Aryan. When the Aryan, bewildered in his reasonings, turns round and says, "There is no God!" the Shemite, hearing him, answers, "God exists. I know him personally. I have talked with him, and he has talked with me." And the Shemitic affirmation of faith has always carried the day against the Aryan suggestion of doubt. For whenever, in the great march of mankind—humanity—the collective Adam[4]—from the mystical Eastern gate of Eden, an Aryan religion has come in contact with a Shemitic religion, the Aryan religion has at once gone to the wall, waned pale, wilted, and subsided.

In the year 606 B.C., Nebuchadnezzar, the Shemitic King of Shemitic-Hamitic Babylon, utterly and definitively defeated Joachim, the

---

[4] Saint Paul, that great Kabbalist, shows clearly (*Romans* v. 12–19; and 1 *Corinthians* xiv. 22), that by the word "Adam" is to be understood the original *Collective Man*. The Collective Man may very well have once existed in a single person, or, rather, in a single couple; and, in fact, tradition informs us that it has twice so existed—once in Adam and Eve, and once in Noah and his wife.

Shemitic king of Shemitic Jerusalem, and transplanted the mass of the Jewish people, as captives, to the neighborhood of Babylon.

During their captivity, the chiefs of the Jews, already initiated into the profound mysteries of the Hebrew religion, were further initiated into the occult science of the Chaldeans—a science of Hamitic origin, akin to that of Tyre and Sidon, and to that which had its mysterious colleges on Mount Gebal.

About seventy years after the fall of Jerusalem, Cyrus, king of the Turanian and Aryan Medes, and of the Aryan Persians, having first turned the Euphrates aside, took Babylon by storm, on the night of a drunken and frantic Chaldean festival. He entered the city by the way of the empty river-bed, bringing with him, as official chaplains of his army, the more illustrious of the Median Magi, and the Aryan chief-priests of Ormudz.

The captive Jews, who had been all along conspirators in Babylon, and secret allies of the Persians, furnished guides, spies and scouts to the invading Aryan army. After the taking of the city, Cyrus rewarded the Jews with his personal friendship, and sent them back to their own country, with instructions to rebuild Jerusalem; which latter city remained, after its restoration, for several generations, as much from gratitude as policy, a Persian stronghold.

At the solemn conferences that took place in the East of Babylon, near the great Tower, at the time of the Persian conquest, between the Median Magi, the Chaldean soothsayers, the Aryan priests of Ormudz, and the Hebrew Prophets, the facts were clearly verified, that, on one side, man aspires towards God, and, on the other, that the Supreme condescends to take up his abode, and to utter his oracles, in the secret temple of the human heart. These facts had, it is true, been well known for centuries to the generality of simple

---

[5] "This commandment which I command thee this day, it is not hidden from thee, neither is it far off. It is not in heaven, that thou shouldest say, Who shall go up for us to heaven, and bring it unto us, that we may hear it, and do it. Neither is it beyond the sea, that thou shouldest say, Who shall go over the sea for us, and bring it unto us, that we may hear it, and do it. But the word is very nigh unto thee, in thy mouth, and in thy heart, that thou mayest do it."—*Deut.* xxx. 11–14

and pious men and women in private station, and also to prophets[5] and inspired poets; but they had never before been so verified to the conviction of kings and statesmen, in the presence of concurring and confessing sacerdotal corporations.

At these conferences, the three constituent elements of the universal consciousness of the collective Adam, were severally and respectively represented. The Aryan priests of Ormudz maintained the claims of the *object* in thought. The Hamitic-Chaldean soothsayers (Hamitic Egypt had no delegate at the synod) maintained the claims of the human *subject*. And the Hebrew Prophets from the Holy Land maintained the claims of the *relation* which subsists between the subject and the object in thought. For, where the Aryan *sees* inwardly, and affirms the reality of the *object*, and the Shemite *hears* inwardly, and affirms the reality of the *relation* between the subject and the object, the Hamite *feels* inwardly, but very darkly, and affirms the reality of the human *subject*.[6]

In these conferences were also verified the foundations of that sublime and universal science, which, six centuries afterwards, was published among adepts, as the Holy Kabbalah, and which had been known, but fragmentarily only, and in its essential principles, long before, to men of the stamp of Abraham, Zoroaster, Moses, Solomon king of Jerusalem, and Hiram king of Tyre.

The Orient of Babylon was not intellectually competent to co-ordinate the principles of the Kabbalah, and to present the completed synthetic doctrine in a definitive form. There was a necessity that the materials should remain unsystematized until the human intellect could have an opportunity to become sharpened by the practice of Greek metaphysical dialectics. Many Greek words occur in the *Zohar,* or Book of Splendor; and it is difficult to believe

---

[6] Of course, the synod took no cognizance of the metaphysical distinction of the subject, the object, and the relation, in thought, under its modern abstract form. What we now call the *object*, was then darkly cognized as the Japhetic characteristic, tendency, and inspiring natural principle; what we call the *subject*, as the Hamitic characteristic, tendency, and inspiring natural principle; and what we call the *relation*, as the Shemitic, &c.

that certain essential passages of the *Idra Suta* (the third tract in the collection of the lesser *Zohar*) could have been written by any one unacquainted with Aristotle's treatise of Metaphysics.[7] Careful investigators have decided, from what they regard as internal evidence, that the definitive compilation of the Kabbalah dates from some period between the year 200 B.C. and the year 150 of the Christian era. It is the internal form of the Kabbalah, however, its substance only, that is systematic: its exposition in words has been left, apparently with deliberate intention, in an exceedingly chaotic state. To the majority of readers, the Kabbalah is, as it ought to be, completely unintelligible.

✸✸✸

At an unknown and remote epoch, it was affirmed, probably by some Hamite, as a postulate of faith, that God and man are in the same likeness or image. It was also affirmed, as a logical consequence of this fundamental affirmation, (1) that, since man is triune, the Supreme is also triune, and (2) that, since man may be denoted by an ascending triangle, the Supreme may be denoted by a descending triangle. The figure in the margin is not at all idolatrous; for it is not, as ABRAK is, a disguised image or likeness. It is a reminder only—a sign or symbol—not a resemblance. It is a pictorial *word*, suggesting a thought—such as were in common and necessary use before the alphabet was invented.

It was also affirmed, perhaps at the same unknown epoch, that the interlacing of the Divine triangle with the human triangle, in the six-rayed Blazing Star, is the authentic symbol of the

---

[7] "The thought which is most, is thought concerning that which is most: and mind knows itself through the perception of that which is intelligible; and mind becomes intelligible to itself through reflection and thought: so that intelligence itself becomes intelligible. . . . Thus God possesses in perfection what we possess for a time only. He possesses more than we have stated; for he possesses, is addition, life. The action of intelligence is life; and God is that action."—*Aristotle's Metaphysics*, Book xii.

revelation of God to man, and of the abode of the Supreme in the human heart, as well as of the aspiration of man towards God. Jacob Behmen asserts that the junction of these two triangles is the most significant and mystical figure in nature. The reality denoted by this symbol is neither God nor man: it is distinct from man, before him, and above him, as the human Ideal; and it is apart from God, as one of the Revelations of Himself that the Supreme sees fit to make to man—as one of the NAMES of Him who, in his own essence, is NAMELESS.

Sometimes the six-rayed Blazing Star is portrayed as a mystic Rose with six leaves. But the ordinary form is that of the two interlacing triangles, with the Divine NAME inscribed in the middle of the figure. The interlacing triangles are often indicated by a junction of the square and compasses: to which, sometimes, the plumb and the level are added, forming a cross in the centre, and giving a ten-rayed Star, with four of the rays (those formed by the extremities of the plumb and level) occulted. This is the *prophetic* Star; and the ten rays stand for the ten Kabbalistic Sephiroth. Without a preliminary understanding of the ten Sephiroth, the Kabbalah, as a Philosophy of History, and consequently as a Practical Art for the forecasting of future events, cannot be appreciated.

We will do our best at some future time, if occasion offers, to explain these ten rays, ray by ray, from the Kabbalistic point of view.

✳✳✳

The ordinary, every-day man or woman, that is to say, the man or woman who has not yet reached perfection—and who is there that has reached perfection?—may be symbolically represented, if he or she be morally of age, by an equilateral triangle with one angle pointing upward to the Blazing Star. Whoso recognizes the virtue of that Star, at once acknowledges the Divine Law in its threefold applications, and strives after conformity with the Ideal, not according to the spirit only, but also according to the soul and the body.

Man's duty to himself and to his fellow-man, under the rays of the Blazing Star, is threefold: (1) the achievement of his own Liberty; (2) the definitive establishment of relations of Equality between himself and other men; and (3) the fusion of himself, in the solidarity of Brotherhood, with all human beings who, like himself, recognize the Blazing Star.

LIBERTY is the power which every human being ought to possess of acting according to the dictates of his own private conscience, under the rays of that Blazing Star which is seen by him, secretly, from the centre of his individual heart.

EQUALITY is the condition that obtains in every society where no special or artificial privilege is granted to any one, or to any set, of its members.

BROTHERHOOD is that strict solidarity between the members of a social body, which causes, under the rays of the Blazing Star, the welfare of each to be seen as involved in that of every other, and of all, and that of all in that of each.

Liberty is the right of each member against every other member, and against all the members. Equality is the right of every other member, and of all the members, against each member. Liberty and Equality find their harmony in the synthetic principle of Fraternity. LIBERTY, EQUALITY, FRATERNITY: this is the mystical triangle that ought to be inscribed on the banners of every truly-constituted social organism.

Liberty alone may lead to anarchy, or to the tyranny of individuals over the mass; but the dangers from Liberty vanish in the presence of Equality. Equality alone may lead to the tyranny of the general mass over individuals or over minorities; but the dangers from Equality vanish in the presence of Liberty. Fraternity is never alone; for it is, in its essence; the synthesis of Liberty and Equality.

★★★

What is it to be a SLAVE? It is to have the inward knowledge of that which is great and holy, and to be constrained to do things that are small and base. It is to be a person consciously capable of self-government, and to be, at the same time, subject to the will of another person. It is to be a full-grown person whose actual rights are those of a child only. It is to see the Blazing Star, and not be permitted to follow it.

Slavery is a factitious and arbitrarily-imposed prolongation of the term of moral minority. Paternal government, actual or constructive, is just and legitimate when exercised over persons who are morally under age; but, to such as know the Blazing Star, it is, when exercised to the confiscation of their initiative, the most infernal of all tyrannies. Paternal government, exercised by the natural father over his own minor children, is tempered by affection, and justifies itself; but paternal government, exercised by usurpers over their natural equals and superiors, is an oppressive wrong, and the most intolerable of all outrages—at the least, it is so in the estimation of such as have seen the Blazing Star.

It is neither the experience of physical want and privation, nor the fact of subordination to legitimate authority, that makes a man to be a slave; for saints and soldiers suffer hardships, and obey their superiors, and are not slaves. On the contrary, it is by the token of the conscious moral penury which a soul feels when it finds itself helpless and hopeless under the domination of an alien soul—it is by the sentiment of a confiscated individuality, by the consciousness of being annexed, as a base appendage, to another soul—it is by the consciousness of being sacrificed to a foreign personality—it is by the darkening of the moral firmament, and by the occultation of the Blazing Star, through the intervention of an extraneous usurping will—that a man comes to know that he is a slave. And it is, on the other hand, the insolent, lying hypocrisy, the false professions of morality, the transparently-spurious philanthropy, the limitless and blinding arrogance of self-conceit, under which the usurper half-conceals, half-reveals, his unnatural lust to wipe out human souls, and to obliterate every individuality except his own—that gives energy to slaves, and renders conspiracies, risings, strikes, and revolutions, deadly and chronic.

The fundamental right of a man is the right to be himself; and this right is his sovereignty. No man has a right to confiscate the sovereignty of any other man. No man can delegate to another man, or to society, any right which he does not himself possess. A man may wickedly forfeit his sovereignty by the commission of crime; he may perversely turn his back upon the Blazing Star, and abdicate his individuality and his manhood. But no man can *rightfully* abdicate his sovereignty. It is the duty of every man of sane mind, who supports himself, and is not convicted of crime, to vindicate his essential dignity as rightful sovereign of himself and of every thing that pertains to his individuality. Every able-bodied man has a natural right, and a natural duty, to forcibly repel, and to combine with others to forcibly repel, any and all wrongful invasions of his sovereignty. Society exists for the individual, and not the individual for society. Institutions are made for man, and not man for institutions.

✳✳✳

The French Free Masons claim, in their Constitutions, that the formula LIBERTY, EQUALITY, FRATERNITY, has been, from the beginning, the device of their order.

The writer of these pages is, and has been for many years, a member of one of the Masonic Lodges (we are told there were a hundred and twenty of them) that recently planted their banners, under the fire of the Versailles troops, upon the ramparts in front of Paris. He knows not by what authority the demonstration was made. He supposes, however, that it was made by the authority of the Paris Lodges only, and that the consent of the Grand Orient of France was neither requested nor deemed necessary.

It is easy, at this moment, to apply abusive epithets, either to the Commune or to its enemies. The Great Architect of the Universe will, at the proper time, judge both parties.

The French word *commune* is the equivalent of our English word *town*. The word *communiste* may denote, in French, either (1) an advocate of the doctrine that women and property ought to be held in common, or (2) an upholder of the principle of municipal self-government. The Commune of Paris fought, in its recent great fight, not for a community of women and goods, but for municipal self-government. It was well known, both at Paris and at Versailles, while the fighting was going on, that M. Thiers could have made peace with the insurgents, at any moment, by simply guaranteeing to the city of Paris an amount of municipal liberty equal to that which has always been enjoyed by the city of Boston. This fact, which cannot with any plausibility be denied, and which probably will not be denied, suffices, of itself alone, to put the merits of the dispute between the Commune of Paris and the Versailles government, in its true light, and to fully expose the calumnious misrepresentations of the Versailles party.

We are of the opinion, that, taking fighting as it rises, the Commune made a passably good fight. We are especially proud of the heroic women with whom the honor of arms has definitively rested.

We, nevertheless, take the liberty to recommend the Commune to be more circumspect, hereafter, in the matter of summary executions. Better things were expected of the Commune than of the Versailles government; for the Commune represents advancing civilization, while the Versailles government represents the commercial, industrial, and financial feudalism of the present and the past. It will never do for men who have seen the Blazing Star, to follow evil examples, and meet murder with murder. The execution of spies and traitors, and the use of petroleum for incendiary purposes,[8] are perfectly justifiable under the laws of war; but the civilized world does not look with approval, and ought not to look with approval, upon the military execution of priests and other non-combatants. We know (or, at the least, we have been informed) that the Commune offered to exchange the Archbishop of Paris for Blanqui, and that the offer was not accepted. This fact (if it be a fact) consigns

---

[8] We should like to know whether the Union Army, acting under orders, did, or did not, ever set fire to any thing in the valley of the Shenandoah; and whether shells loaded with incendiary composition were, or were not, thrown from our ships and batteries into the city of Charleston.

the memory of M. Thiers to the execration of posterity; but it does not excuse the Commune.

The existing French Assembly was elected, not at all to govern France, but to consult on the possibilities of a reconciliation between France and Prussia, and also, if advisable, to conclude and authenticate a treaty of peace. The Assembly has, therefore, no lawful governmental powers. When the treaty of peace between France and Prussia was signed, the mandate of the Assembly expired. The government of M. Thiers is a government of usurpers. It has belligerent rights, and it has no other rights. Consequently, every disarmed prisoner of war, male or female, shot in cold blood after a combat, in pursuance of M. Thiers's policy, whether sentenced or not sentenced by court-martial, is—from a legal point of view—simply a person assassinated. And the moral aspect of the question is coincident with the legal aspect. If the Communists committed excesses (and it seems they were human), they did so in defending themselves, their families, and their homes, against thieves and usurpers. Thiers fought to confiscate the liberties and control the money of the people of Paris; and Paris fought in defense of the natural rights of its own people.

Three times the heroic people of Paris have been cheated out of their Republic: once in the great revolution; afterwards in 1830; and, again, in 1848. To-day the scales are still oscillating, and the result is yet undetermined. In the next great fight, or in the fight after the next, the Republic will prevail. The Blazing Star as Paris sees it, now struggling with obscurantism and secular wrong, tinges the whole horizon of the East with the glories of the coming day. The Kabbalistic synthesis is nearer than it was!

✶✶✶

The Shemitic principle and the Japhetic principle are to-day represented in human civilization—the first by the Israelitish Church, and the second by the Christian Church. Both of these Churches are true Churches, and therefore neither of them is capable of erring in things essential. The Blazing Star burns in both of them: the junction of the two triangles, one Divine and the other human—the regeneration of the individual soul—takes effect in both of them. Yet these two Churches excommunicate each other! Why? Because these Churches are two Churches only, and not three. Because one whole side of the mystical triangle is lacking in modern civilization. Because the Hamitic principle is to-day occulted. Because the Hamitic Church is nowhere visibly organized, and speaking with authority, among men. Because Man, the natural mediator between heaven and earth, is officially absent from the religious organizations of the period.

Now there are three holy cities—not two of them only: JERUSALEM, ROME, PARIS. But the holiness of Paris is virtual merely as yet. The religion of Humanity reaches higher than the Commune and the International Labor Union seem to think, Paris is *Bar-Isis*, *Parisis*, *Paris*. It is the sacred boat of Isis that bears to-day the destinies of the world.

BROOKLINE, MASS., July, 1871.

THE KABBALAH

THE two kabbalistic[1] books that are of note are the JETSIRAH (the Book of the Creation) and the ZOHAR. The Zohar is *The Book of Splendor*—the book of "the shining ones" of whom it is written, "They that are wise *shall shine* (יזהרו, *zhr-u*) as the *shining* (כזהר, *k-zhr*) of the firmament"—*Dan.* xii. 3.

The Talmud[2] (the authoritative compendium for doctrine and practice among the orthodox Jews) directs that the theory of the creation (or the contents of the book Jetsirah) shall never be taught to two persons at once; and the explanation of the mystical chariot described by the prophet Ezekiel (or the contents of the book Zohar) not even to one, unless he be a man of approved wisdom, and then by a summary of the chapters only.

The most important, and probably the best authenticated, of the documents forming the collection of the Zohar, are the *Siphra de Zeniutha* (the Book of Occultations, or of Mysteries), the *Idra Rabba* (the Greater Assembly), and the *Idra Suta* (the Smaller Assembly). These three short treatises are said by experts to contain the whole real substance of the Kabbalah; and taken together, in the order just mentioned, they form the collection known as *the lesser Zohar*. In point of fact, however, the whole substance of the Kabbalah is contained in the Zeniutha; for the Idra Rabba and the Idra Suta consist of explanations and developments of the doctrines that are darkly outlined in the Book of Mysteries. The last paragraph of the Zeniutha stands as follows:

> Thus far, the Book of the King, or of Mysteries, or of Occultations, remains involved and hidden. Happy is that man who goes in and comes out, and learns its paths and its crossways.

---

[1] קבלה, KABBALAH, that which is *received* (by tradition).
[2] The TALMUD is that which is *taught* (with authority).

The lesser Zohar is written in a corrupt Hebrew idiom, long ago consigned to utter disuse, called "the Jerusalem dialect." Its three tracts, as we now possess them in the printed editions, are accompanied by Latin translations; and in the light thrown by the text on the translations, and by the translations on the text, with the aid afforded by the internal harmonies of the doctrine expounded, some parts of the expositions (if they may be called expositions) become distinctly intelligible.

There are many treatises in French, Latin, and in other languages, nearly all of them easily accessible, containing general accounts of the kabbalistic doctrine, summaries of the various fragments of the Jetsirah and the Zohar, with explanations of the signs, symbols, and of the language generally, of the Kabbalah; giving also practical directions for magical processes, the interpretation of mysteries, the exercise of the prophetic art, and other like matters of interest. Whether the kabbalistic books themselves are harder to understand than the books written to explain them, or the converse, we do not assume to judge: we incline, however, to the suspicion, that, apart from the difficulties of mere language, the commentaries are harder than the text.

The Book of Mysteries opens very obscurely, as follows:

> The Book of Occultations (or of Mysteries) is the book
> of weighing in the Balance. Before this Balance was, face
> (the lesser aspect) answered not back to face (the greater
> aspect). [The Microprosopus looked not back upon the
> Macroprosopus.] And the ancient[3] kings (the symbolical
> kings of Edom, or the worlds that were first created, but
> could not subsist) were dead, and their sustenance was

---

[3] קדמאין, *Kdmain, eastern*. Because the morning in the *east* is anterior to the noon in the *south*, and to the evening in the *west*, the word *eastern* came, from very ancient times, to signify *anteriority*, whether natural or metaphysical. Thus the phrase, "the eastern kings" denoted either the first kings in point of time, or the principiating kings. The "ancient kings" of the text are principiating kings.

> nowhere found, and the earth was desolate (void, existing potentially only), until the non-cognizable Head prepared vestments of honor, and bestowed them upon that which is longed for in all desires (or until the Holy One assumed the form and nature which involves all natures, and maintains them all). This Balance hangs in the place which exists not. Things which appear not are weighed in it. It is composed of that body which is neither compacted nor seen. In it have ascended, and do now ascend, things which are not, and are, and shall be. Occultation in occultation.—*The Zeniutha,* chap. 1 § 1 to § 9.

The *Masora* is in every respect the converse of the Kabbalah. The Masora is that which was openly *delivered* by the Rabbi: the Kabbalah is that which was secretly and mysteriously *received* by the disciple.

There was for the Kabbalah, as there is for every thing else that grows up under the protection of silence and darkness, a long period of incubation. Symbols presented themselves from time to time to the minds of ingenious men, and went into occult circulation among adepts. Some of these symbols were illustrative pictures addressed to the eye, and others of them were enigmatic stories and descriptions addressed to the ear. Century after century passed away before the doctrine took its systematic and definitive form. When the books came to be written, they were written, not to teach the doctrine, but to furnish such a series of arbitrary mnemonic signs as would enable the initiated reader to hold the whole general theory, divided and subdivided into its constituent parts, in one view before his mind. It is in vain, therefore, that a man opens a kabbalistic book, if he have not beforehand, and without the aid of the book, mastered the whole substance of its contents. The books furnish, not matter of teaching, but enigmatic reminders of information already acquired. Moreover, the kabbalistic writers, aiming to conceal rather than to reveal their doctrine, affect preposterousness of statement.

When Rabbi Simon ben Jochai read (*Gen.* iii. 3), "And they heard the voice of the Lord God walking in the garden in the cool of the

day," he refused to believe the things literally stated in the passage.[4]
He reasoned thus: "The passage has a meaning; for it was written
by the author of the *Bereshith*:[5] the literal meaning is not the true
one; for the literal meaning is absurd: the passage has, therefore,
some occult meaning, and that occult meaning is a proper subject
for investigation." Rabbi Simon and the other kabbalistic writers
appear to imitate, in their own expositions, what they suppose to
have been the enigmatic method of the author of the Bereshith.

The Zohar is an explanation of the mystic chariot (מרכבה,
Merkebah) that is described in the first chapter of Ezekiel. The
prophet Ezekiel, when he was among the captives which were by
the River Chebar, saw visions of God. These visions were obviously enigmatic. The prophet saw "a fire infolding itself," and in
the midst of it "the likeness of four living creatures." He saw also
"wheels," the work of which was, "as it were, a wheel within a
wheel." "The rings of the wheels were full of eyes." He saw also
"a firmament" over the wheels and the living creatures, and the
color thereof was "as the color of *the terrible crystal*;" and on this
covering "was the appearance of a throne of sapphire-stone," and
"upon the likeness of the throne was the likeness of the appearance
of a MAN above upon it."[6] "And the appearance of the brightness
round about it was as the appearance of the bow that is in the cloud
in the day of rain," or as the appearance of light when it is passing through transparent crystal.—*Ezek.* chap. i. We read, furthermore—but this time it is the prophet Daniel who sees the vision—"I
beheld till the thrones were cast down, and the Ancient of days did
sit, whose garment was white as snow, and the hair of his head
like pure wool: his throne was like the fiery flame, and his wheels

---

[4] R. Simon ben Jochai is mentioned by several of the kabbalistic writers as the
master who reduced the Kabbala to its definitive form.

[5] The Bereshith (בראשית, *In the beginning*) is the first part of the first book
of the Hebrew Bible.

[6] "Then went up Moses and Aaron, Nadab and Abihu, and seventy of the elders
of Israel (into the mount). And they saw the God of Israel; and there was under
his feet as it were a *paved work of a sapphire-stone*, and as it were the body of
heaven in its clearness."—*Exod.* xxiv. 9, 10.

as burning fire."—*Dan.* vii. 9. A parallel vision is recorded in the Apocalypse, where the meaning is, however, somewhat obscured through the rendering of the term ζωα (*zoa*, living creatures) by the unfortunate term "beasts." Ezekiel says (x. 20), "This is the *living creature* that I saw under the God of Israel by the river of Chebar; *and I knew that they were the cherubim.*"

The author of the Zeniutha,[7] having realized the vision of the Merkebah in his imagination, expresses himself in the following extraordinary language:

> The non-cognizable Head is framed and prepared (or is to be conceived) after the similitude of a skull (1) filled with crystalline dew (2). The covering membrane (3) of this skull is completely transparent, and closed; and from it hair (4 and 5) like white wool hangs on either side in equilibrium.[8]
>
> The supreme (6) Loving-kindness (the forehead of the Macroprosopus) reveals itself to the prayers of that which is below.
>
> Open Vision (the eyes of the Macroprosopus) slumbering never, but observing continually (7 and 8).
>
> In the superior aspect (the Macroprosopus) are two apertures (the nostrils), through which the spirit (9) is called forth in all.
>
> The aspect which is below (10) answers to the aspect of the superior lights.
>
> "In the beginning, God created the heavens and the earth."—*Gen.* i. 1. Six (שתא, *shetha*) created six (שית

---

[7] Rabbi Simon indicates very clearly, in the Idra Suta, that he himself was the author of the Zeniutha.

[8] This figure, or symbol, is offensive to the imagination. It ought to be so. The writers of the Kabbala intentionally select emblems that are absurd, in bad taste, and utterly inadequate. Their emblems are mnemonic signs, or reminders, not illustrations. Apt and beautiful symbols almost always give occasion to idolatrous practices. The Kabbala is so written that the mind of the intelligent adept is repelled by the sign, and passes at once to the consideration of the thing signified.

ברא, *bara-shih*). Upon these (six) depend all things that are below. For that which is below depends upon the influences which are the Head's beard; but the second earth (the actual world) counts not among the six. The existing earth is produced from another earth that bore the curse: as it is written (*Gen.* v. 21), "From the ground which the Lord had cursed."

"And the earth was without form, and void" (תהו ובהו, *thohu va bohu*, a collective potentiality of existence in a potentiality of existence); "and darkness was upon the face of the deep" (תהום, *thehom*, the Abyss).—*Gen.* i. 2.

Thirteen (below) answer to the thirteen (influences of the beard). Six thousand years (six numerations, or sephiroth, of the Microprosopus) answer to the six first (the six of the Macroprosopus). The seventh thousand years (the seventh numeration or sephirah after the third, or Matrona, or Royalty) is apart, and over that which is vehement, and vehement only.

And all was desolate for twelve hours—the hours in which the earth was formless and empty. But the vehemency was reconstructed in the thirteenth hour through mercy, and renewed. And all six persisted; for it is written, "He *created*;" and afterwards it is written, "And the earth *was*:" so that the vehemency was a subsisting *reality* (although not an *actuality* even while existing potentially only).—*The Zeniutha*, chap. i. § 10 to § 24.

These extracts are supposed to contain the essence of the Kabbalah. We have translated them as we could, feeling our way darkly; and are confident that our interpretation is not very far from right.

What is this Balance which hangs in the place that exists not, bearing in its scales things that are not, and are, and shall be? What is this Supreme Form (or nature) that involves all forms (or natures), and maintains them all? Who are these Kings of Edom that *are*, but *exist not*? What are these Living Creatures, these man-headed, lion-headed, ox-headed, and eagle-headed Sphinxes, darkly referred to in the text, and of which the prophet Ezekiel says openly, "I knew that they were the Cherubim"? It is more than possible that we may fail to give adequate answers to these questions. But the plan of our undertaking does not require that our answers should be adequate. The passages of which a rendering has been submitted to the reader mean something; for Simon ben Jochai was the writer of them. Their obvious meanings are manifold, and destroy each other. The statements are obviously, therefore, *enigmatic*. It shall be our effort to give in a plain way, and in the ordinary language of metaphysics, such necessarily inadequate answers to the above-recited questions, and such partial interpretations of the enigmas contained in the extracts, as will enable us to set forth, in a more or less satisfactory manner, the kabbalistic theory of the TEN SEPHIROTH. This was the task we assigned to ourselves in the beginning. We shall say very little of those parts of the doctrine that are protected to-day by sworn obligations. Let no initiate be frightened beforehand! We shall also fortify our own expositions with copious extracts from the Idra Rabba and the Idra Suta, in order that our readers may be convinced that we say what the Kabbalah says, and are not passing off false coin upon them. Our readers will, necessarily, be few in number; and for that reason, if for no other, we intend to treat them fairly. The Zohar says,

> Sometimes two Mekubbalim are found in the same city, and seven in a kingdom: at other times, only one is found in a city, and only two in a whole generation.

Nevertheless, the books of the Kabbalah have been continually republished, first by oral tradition from generation to generation, and then by expensive printed edition after expensive printed edition, for the benefit of the few who care for them: so that the doctrine has come down, almost intact, even to the present day.

THE KABBALISTIC BALANCE

Man knows himself to be soul and body, spontaneity and fatality, subject and object, spirit and matter.

Spontaneity and fatality—the first regarded as *masculine,* or initiative; and the second as *feminine,* or responsive—are the two scales of that Universal Balance in which all things are weighed. It is written in the Zohar:

> When the Most Holy Elder, hidden in all occultations, willed to create, *he made all things in the form of husband and wife,* conditioning the existence of opposite sexes.—*Idra Suta,* § 218. Wisdom (חכמה, *Chochmah*) is the Father: Understanding (בינה, *Binah*) is the Mother. Wisdom and Understanding are weighed IN ONE BALANCE, as male and female.—*Id. Sut.,* § 222. *All things appear, therefore, in the form of husband and wife: were it otherwise, nothing whatever could subsist.—Id. Sut.,* § 223. And this Father and Mother are called *the house:* as it is written (*Prov.* xxiv. 3), "Through Wisdom is a house builded, and by Understanding it is established."—*Id. Sut.,* § 312. The male is a mere half-body: so also the female.—*Id. Sut.,* § 718. Blessings descend not upon mutilated and defective things, but upon that which is complete—not upon half-things.—*Id. Sut.,* § 723. Half-things neither subsist in eternity, nor receive blessings for eternity.—*Id. Sut.,* § 724.

Heaven and Earth, the State and the Church, the Emperor and the Pope, Liberty and Authority, Revolution and Order, the Law and the Gospel, Private Opinion and Public Opinion, the Intuitive Method and the Inductive Method, Poetry and Prose, Spontaneity and Fatality, Subject and Object, Spirit and Matter, and the like, are weighed, each over against its correlative, in that Universal Balance which is Man and Woman, or rather Husband and Wife.

Sometimes, in examining a kabbalistic couple, we find it difficult to determine which term is husband, and which is wife; but the Kabbalah furnishes a test. The Zohar says,

> All rigors that rise in the male are vehement in the beginning, and relaxed at the end: those, however, that rise in the female, are mild in the beginning, but vehement at the end.—*Idra Rabba*, § 1026. And, were it not that these are conjoined, the world would not be able to bear them. The Elder of elders, therefore, separates them from each other, and then associates them that they may assuage each other.—*Id. Rab.*, § 1027.

Applying this test, we judge (with, however, many misgivings) that Heaven is masculine, and the Earth feminine; the State masculine, and the Church feminine; the Emperor masculine, and the Pope feminine; and so on.

The rigor that rises in the male, and that which rises in the female, subsist in the analogy of correlative opposites. Each implies the other, is related to the other; and either, without the other, would be unprovoked, unmeaning, nonexistent, and void. Each is, however, a mystery to the other; and each, in affirming itself, excludes the other: so that the two, unassuaged, stand as a subsisting contradiction. This contradiction is resolved when the two are weighed against each other in the Balance, and mutuality takes the place of reciprocal isolation. In the Balance, like repels like, and union is established between contraries. The theory of the Balance is, therefore, the theory of the reconciliation of contradictions. Now, there cannot be two hills without a valley between them; for, if there be no valley, the hills are not two hills, but the same hill. Absolute contradiction (or the affirmation that the same thing in the same subject both is and is not) is a sign of nullity. If the same thing could be at the same time both true and not true, and in the same sense, it would be useless for man to seek after truth. Kabbalistic contradictions subsist, therefore, never absurdly in a single term, but always in two terms that answer each other: they are always relative, and never absolute. It is only when two affirmations imply each other as well as deny each other, assert each other as well as exclude each other, that we know we are in the presence of a contradiction-pregnant, and on the eve of discovering a third term, in which the two discordant terms will find their synthetic harmony. Furthermore, a single affirmation of a contradiction being given, and not both of them, it is only when the given affirmation, carefully considered, presents its own refutation, and when the refutation, in its turn, re-affirms the original proposition, that we have the promise of a coming synthesis.

The Kabbalah affirms that all things are constructed, and held in being, in accordance with the principle of the contradiction-pregnant. "Before the Balance was, face answered not to face, and the earth was void." It follows, therefore, if the Kabbalah be true, that the method of contradictions is the authentic method of philosophic and scientific investigation.

We permit ourselves to remark, in this place, that a man ought never to be regarded as being substantially the same thing as a woman, or a woman as substantially the same thing as a man, each existing as the other, but with defect: for men and women are kabbalistic correlatives of each other, not defects of each other; and their essential value consists in their sharp reciprocal contradistinction from each other.

Men and women ought always to be kabbalistically united with each other in synthetic marriage, and never joined in simple partnership. Our women's-rights people are wholly wrong in this particular. Man divorced from woman, religion from science, love from knowledge, force from gentleness, pity from justice, and the converse, are worse than barren: they are destructive. Every kabbalistic couple should be regarded as a true couple, not as two varieties of the same thing. Men and women are analogies of each other, not aspects of each other. The opposing terms of such couples should be contradistinguished, not that a choice may be made between them, not that one may be sacrificed to the other, or subjugated by the other, but that both may be accepted, and the two weighed against each other in the Balance in actual marriage; for, in the kabbalistic marriage, we obtain distinction without antagonism, union without uniformity, order without despotism, and a complete analysis resolved by a complete synthesis. So long as the two terms of a kabbalistic couple stand unreconciled, they are the occasion of sorrow, suffering, want, oppression, and wrong; they are the material itself of evil: but, as soon as they are married, they generate and bring forth harmony and beauty.

We have been able, but under cover of much darkness, to set forth, thus far, the theory of the Kabbalistic Balance. In this Balance the whole doctrine of the Zohar hangs. As we go on with our exposition, the theory will become, by degrees, clearer and clearer.

Harmony subsists by the resolution of contraries. Analogy is either sameness of law with diversity of attributes, or it is diversity of law with sameness of attributes. Analogy is the key that unlocks the secret of the universe. An effort that wastes itself in the void counts not at all. That, and that only, supports, which also resists. He that suffers, grows; he that enjoys, wilts. Prosperity is harder to bear than adversity. Evil and wrong should provoke pity, not anger. So long as man shall remain progressive in his nature, evil will be a condition of his existence. Evil is necessary. Injustice, hostility, disappointment, want, obscurity, and neglect discipline human spontaneity, and enable it to assert its own.

In disputed questions of faith, the kabbalist espouses both sides of the controversy. To the kabbalist, the doctrine of irresistible grace on the one side; and of man's responsibility on the other, which arrays the Calvinists against the followers of Arminius, and the converse, is nothing other than a contradiction-pregnant susceptible of strict scientific solution. The first virtue of a wise man is that of entire toleration of opinions. All men know partially and defectively. A few men know both sides of certain special questions. The Supreme, and he only, knows the whole.

THE CHERUBIM

The word *cherub*[9] is complex, technical, and artificial. It is composed arbitrarily of two elements: one signifying the act of carving, or engraving;[10] and the other signifying multitudinousness.[11] The cherubim of the tabernacle were not, as might be supposed from the analysis of the word, carved, or graven, images, but were images that had been hammered into shape. It is written (*Exod.* xxv. 13),

> Thou shalt make two cherubim of gold; *of beaten work* shalt thou make them, in the two ends of the mercy-seat.

The cherubim of the temple were, however, of carved work; for it is written (1 *Kings* vi. 23–29),

> And, within the oracle, Solomon made two cherubim *of olive-tree*, each ten cubits high. . . . And he overlaid the cherubim with gold. And he carved all the walls of the house round about *with carved figures of cherubim* and palm-trees and open flowers, within and without.

The following extract from Layard's "Nineveh" (vol. ii. p. 352) will sufficiently describe the external form of the kabbalistic cherubim:

> Ezekiel saw in his vision the likeness of four living creatures, which had four faces, four wings, and the hands of a man under their wings on their four sides. Their faces were those of a man, a lion, an ox, and an

---

[9] כרוב, *krub*, cherub.

[10] כר, *kr.* This Hebrew element indicates distinctive marks, gravings, characters; also the act of engraving, and engraving-tools. It is found in the English words *carve* and *engrave*. It also indicates all kinds of excavations, incisions, or pits: hence the English word *grave*.

[11] רב, *rb*, multitude, abundance.

eagle. By them was a wheel, the appearance of which was, as it were, a wheel in the middle of a wheel. It will be observed that the four forms chosen by Ezekiel to illustrate his description—the man, the lion, the bull, and the eagle—are precisely those which are constantly found on Assyrian monuments as religious types.

The prophet Ezekiel says (x. 8–20),

And there appeared in the cherubim the form of a man's hand under their wings. . . . And every one had four faces: the first face was the face of a cherub (or of an ox: compare i. 10); and the second face was the face of a man; and the third, the face of a lion; and the fourth, the face of an eagle. . . This is the Living Creature (חיה, *chyh*) that I saw under the God of Israel by the River Chebar; *and I knew that they were the cherubim.*

It is written in the New Testament (*Apoc.* iv. 6, 7),

And in the midst of the throne, and round about the throne, were four beasts (ζωα, *zoa*, living creatures), full of eyes before and behind. And the first beast was like a lion, and the second beast like a calf, and the third beast had a face as a man, and the fourth beast was like a flying eagle.

In art, the evangelist Matthew is usually represented as accompanied by a man; the evangelist Mark, by a lion; the evangelist Luke, by an ox; and the evangelist John, by an eagle. Thus the kabbalistic cherubim are made to stand as symbols of the four Gospels.

The cherubim described as carved upon the walls of the ideal temple (which was never built) had two faces only—the face of a young lion, and the face of a man.—*Ezek.* xli. 19. It is probable that the golden calf made by Aaron, and the golden calves set up by King Jeroboam—one in Beth-el and the other in Dan—were cherubim.

The general outward aspect of the cherubim is now sufficiently indicated.

The particular four-faced, winged, and flying cherubim of Ezekiel's vision are the kabbalistic cherubim, whose special enigmatic characteristics were probably borrowed by the prophet, as symbols, from the ancient worship of Tyre and Sidon—a worship akin to that of Babylon, but differing from it by being truer to the primitive Hamitic traditions. We will dwell for a moment on this point. We read (*Ezek.* xxviii. 11, 16)—

> The word of the Lord came unto me, saying, Son of man, take up a lamentation upon the king of Tyrus, and say unto him, Thus saith the Lord God: Thou sealest up the sum, exact in number, and perfect in coinage. Thou hast been in Eden, the garden of God: every precious stone was thy covering—the sardius, the topaz, and the diamond; the beryl, the onyx, and the jasper; the sapphire, the emerald, and the carbuncle; and gold. . . . Thou art the anointed cherub that covereth; and I have set thee so. Thou wast upon the holy mountain of God. Thou hast walked up and down in the midst of the stones of fire (or splendor). Thou wast perfect in thy ways from the day that thou wast created, till iniquity was found in thee. By the multitude of thy merchandise thou hast been filled, in the midst of thee, with violence; thou hast sinned: therefore will I cast thee as profane out of the mountain of God; and I will destroy thee, O covering cherub! from the midst of the stones of fire."

Tyre ought certainly to have made common cause, from the beginning, with Jerusalem, against King Nebuchadnezzar, and should never have allowed the two cities to be attacked and overwhelmed in detail. Insanity was epidemic among the kings of the epoch. The king of Tyre insanely identified, in his own mind, the totality of his people, and also his people's god, with his own person. "This, his power, became his god." In the blind egotism of his insanely assumed godhead, he betrayed Jerusalem to her enemies, and thus broke down the barrier that had separated between King Nebuchadnezzar and himself. After the eyes of the king of Tyre had been fully opened, by the experience of events, to the fatal consequences of his own selfish bad faith, the prophet, with, as it were, an instinctive sense of the proper local coloring, taunted him, and insulted him with deliberate purpose. It is not without a sentiment of bitter and pitiless irony, or without a distinct knowledge that the poisoned shaft would hit, that Ezekiel addresses the king of Tyre by the title, "O covering cherub!"

The breastplate of judgment, suspended from the neck of the Jewish high priest, had, in the first row, a topaz, a sardius, and a carbuncle; it had, in the second row, an emerald, a sapphire, and a diamond; in the third row, a ligure, an agate, and an amethyst; and, in the fourth row, a beryl, an onyx, and a jasper. The precious stones that were "the covering" of the king of Tyre, were, as far as they went, the jewels of the breastplate of judgment. The foundation-stones of the wall of the New Jerusalem are as follows: a jasper, sapphire, and a chalcedony; an emerald, a sardonyx, and a sardius; a chrysolite, a beryl, and a topaz; a chrysoprasus, a jacinth, and an amethyst. And the twelve gates are twelve pearls. The chief god of Tyre was represented in the Tyrian temple by a perfectly clear emerald as large as a man's two fists. The worship of stones was still extant in Tyre at the time the prophet wrote.

It now remains for us to determine the symbolical signification of these hammered and graven images, and to discover, if we can, why it was that the meaning *multitudinousness* was made to enter into the very structure of the word *cherub*.

In modern poetical usage, the cherubim appear as *angels*. We may, however, dismiss at once this interpretation of the symbol, since it receives no sanction whatever from Scripture. The Living Creatures of the Apocalypse were obviously not angels; for we read (v. 3-10),

> And, when he had taken the book, the four living creatures (*zoa*) and the four and twenty elders fell down

> before the Lamb: and they sang a new song, saying,
> Thou art worthy to take the book, and to open the
> seals thereof; for thou wast slain, and hast redeemed us
> to God by thy blood *out of every kindred and tongue
> and people and nation*; and hast made us unto our God
> kings and priests, and we shall reign in the earth.

The words, "Out of every nation, kindred, tongue, and people," give us an intimation that the symbolical *Living Creatures*
mentioned in Scripture are complex beings, and that the individuals of which they are composed are nothing other than MEN. The
indication is confirmed by an inspection of the following among
other passages:

> Thou, O God! didst send a plentiful rain, whereby thou
> didst confirm thine inheritance when it was weary. Thy
> *congregation* (חיתך, *chyth-ka*, thy Living Creature)
> hath dwelt therein.—*Ps.* lxviii. 9, 10. And the Philistines
> were gathered together into a *troop* (לחיה, *le-chyeh*,
> into a Living Creature) where was a piece of ground
> full of lentils.—2 *Sam.* xxiii. 11. And *the troop* (חית,
> *chyth*, the Living Creature) of the Philistines pitched in
> the valley of Rephaim.—ver. 13.

The books of grammar say that collective nouns, the names of
kinds and sorts, do not designate realities; but the books of grammar
are not always of authority in matters philosophical. We must divest
ourselves of the prejudice which causes us to see in special societies
nothing but beings of the mind, mere abstract names, serving to designate aggregations of men. There is something in every constituted
society more than the mere aggregate, the mere unity of totality, of
the individuals composing it. Is the state, *quoad* state, nothing? the
church, *quoad* church, nothing? the army, *quoad* army, nothing? the
work-shop, *quoad* an organization of industry, nothing? When, in
the order of Providence, the organic unity of a particular people is
broken, that people finds, to its extreme cost, that a mere aggrega-

tion of individuals never suffices to constitute a people. The voice of the majority of a people, or even the voice of all its individual members, may be something very different from that organic voice of the people which is (said to be) the voice of God. To the true philosopher, society is a LIVING CREATURE, endowed with an intelligence and an activity of its own, governed by special laws, which are discoverable by observation, and by observation only; and whose existence is manifested, not under a material aspect, but by the close concert and the mutual interdependence (the *solidarity*) of all the members of the social body.

The maxim, "The voice of the people is the voice of God," is very ancient. In many of the Shemitic countries, the collective people was the occult god of the individual members of the people. The kings of Assyria continually affected to identify themselves with Asshur, the common ancestor of the whole people, and therefore the symbol of the collective people, and the occult god of the people. Louis XIV said, "I am the state:" the kings of Assyria went farther, and said, "We are Assyria and Asshur." But the claim of the Assyrian kings to divine honors seems to have been always resisted. Self-deification was the form taken by the royal insanity of the period.[12]

A CHERUB is a hammered or graven image that is enigmatically representative of a Living Creature—of *a collective man*. A political meeting is a Living Creature, bearing the likeness of *a man*; for the mass of the assembly is its body, the moderator is its executive faculty, and the orators and managers are the active intelligence. A nation is a Living Creature, whose body is composed of the mass of citizens, whose will is organized in the executive element, whose

---

[12] God standeth in the congregation of the mighty
He judgeth among the gods. . . .
I have said, Ye are gods,
And all of you children of the Most High;
But ye shall die like men,
And fall like one of the princes.
Arise, O God! judge the earth:
For it is thou that shalt inherit all nations.—*Ps.* lxxxii.

intelligence resides in the legislature, and whose active conscience—
that is, whose passions and instinctive tendencies, as tempered
down and rendered permanent by the joint action of the memory
and the legislative judgment—resides in the judiciary. Because the
individuals of a nation become *one* by thus subsisting in relations
of mutual interdependence (of *solidarity*), because they are thus
brought into the form of a collective man, they actually become
a collective entity, capable of collective virtue and crime. Nations
commit national sins. And it cannot be affirmed that the Social
Unity is the result of a social compact; for the actor is always prior
to its acts; and the social compact, since it is the act and product of
the Social Organism, supposes the prior existence of this Organism.
No national constitution can ever be put in operation that does not
exist in the order of Providence, or in that of destiny, before it is
written on paper.

A mature people has, however, no real *personality*. It is only
while a people is in a condition of mental and moral minority, while
it is as yet under age, that it takes to itself—a king or an emperor,
in order that it may theatrically and fictitiously represent itself in
the personality of its executive chief. The madness of a people is
correlative with the madness of its rulers. When a people becomes
mature, its government becomes impersonal. Self-government, or
the government of the organic people, is equivalent to the substitution of responsible administration in the stead of government.
"The best government is that which governs least." A true society, although it is a real entity, although it is a Living Creature,
is never a person.

One of the two cherubim of the tabernacle was an emblematic
representative of the collective body made up of the children of
Leah, and the other was a symbol of the collective body made up
of the children of Rachel. When the high priest entered, once a
year, into the Holy of Holies, and there looked upon the Shechinah
enthroned between the cherubim, he saw the symbol of what met
his eyes, in its reality, when he came back into the camp.

According to the Hebrew religion, Israel was not in the desert
and in Palestine, as Asshur was in Assyria, the occult god of the

people, but was, on the contrary, a mere cherub, having his station under the throne of the God of Israel.[13]

Israel, to the minds of the inspired prophets, was a very mysterious personage. Israel was the father of the nation. Israel was the nation itself—the collective child of Israel. Israel was also the spirit that co-ordinated the mass of the people into one organic whole—into one Living Creature. Israel was Father, Son, and Spirit. In the view of the more inspired of the prophets, Israel, as the Son, as the Israelitish people itself, was a vicarious sacrifice for the nations. It is written (*Isa.* lii. 13–liii. 11),

> Behold, *my servant* shall prosper. . . .
> Many shall be amazed at the sight of him.
> His face is marred more than that of other men;
> And his form is so disfigured as to be scarcely human.
> So shall he deliver *many nations,*
> And kings shall shut their mouths before him. . . .
> He hath no comeliness to draw attention,
> Nor beauty that men should take pleasure in him.
> He is despised and rejected of men;
> A man of sorrows, and acquainted with grief. . . .
> He was wounded for our transgressions,
> And bruised for our iniquities.
> For our peace the chastisement was laid upon him,
> And by his stripes we are healed. . . .
> He shall see the travail of his soul, and be satisfied.
> By his knowledge shall my righteous *servant* justify many;
> For he shall bear their iniquities.

Who is this *servant* that is thus smitten for the welfare of *the nations?* Let the Scriptures themselves answer. It is written (*Isa.* xli. 8, 9),

---

[13] It is supposed that the setting-up of the golden calf in the desert was an attempt to overthrow the true Hebrew religion, and to substitute the worship of the collective Hebrew people, as a cherubic god, in the stead of the worship of Jehovah.

> But thou, O *Israel*! art my *servant*,
> Thou, *Jacob*, whom I have chosen,
> The seed of *Abraham*, my friend—Thou whom I have
> taken from the ends of the earth,
> And called from tha boundaries thereof,
> Saying unto thee, Thou art my *servant*.

And again (xliv. 1, 2),

> Hear now, O *Jacob*, my *servant*,
> And *Israel* whom I have chosen!
> Thus saith Jehovah that made thee,
> That formed thee from the womb, and will help thee:
> Fear not, O *Jacob*, my *servant*—
> Jesurun, whom I have chosen!

And again (xlix. 3),

> Thou art my servant,
> O Israel! in whom I will be glorified.

And again (xlii. 1, 7),

> Behold my *servant*, whom I uphold;
> Mine elect, in whom my soul delighteth!
> I have put my spirit upon him:
> He shall bring forth judgment to *the nations*. . . .
> He shall not fail, nor be discouraged,
> Till he have set justice in the earth;
> And distant *nations* shall wait for his law. . . .
> I, Jehovah, have called thee in righteousness,
> And will hold thee by the hand,
> And will make thee a covenant to the people,
> And a light to the *nations*."

Perhaps the first authentic instance, in recorded literature, of a complete development of the sentiment of universal good will to man, is the one found in the words (*Gen.* xii. 3), "And in thee (Abram) *shall all the families of the earth be blessed*." Israel always regarded itself as the chosen people, but as chosen to be *the Christ of the nations*—the instrument through which the law of Jehovah was to go forth to *all the families of the earth.*

We come now to the turning-point of the Kabbalah—the essence of the Kabbalah. And we request the reader to bear in mind, while he is reading what we are about to say, that the writings of Mr. John Locke and of M. Condillac were not to be found on the shelves of the book-stalls in ancient Tyre, Sidon, Babylon, Jerusalem, and Memphis: if they had been found there, the demand for them would probably have been small. We are disposed to defend nothing and to answer for nothing; for it is our purpose, in this place, to state, to the best of our ability, the extraordinary doctrines of the Kabbalah in their simplest form, to explain them as well as we can, and then leave them to defend themselves.

If Asshur, Mizraim, Israel, Gog, Magog, and the like, are to be recognized as covering cherubs, then much more is ADAM (the collective-man, Humanity) to be recognized as a superior covering cherub. Above the heads of the cherubim, Ezekiel saw in his vision the likeness of a firmament, and over the firmament the appearance of a throne, "and on the throne the likeness of the appearance, as it were, of A MAN." The Kabbalah affirms that the ideal Humanity, the Adam which was from the beginning, before ever the earth was, and who is above, is the First-born of the Ancient of days, and that by him the heavens and the earth were created. The Kabbalah affirms, further, that ADAM—the first Adam, *Adam Kadmon*—unlike other cherubim, has a distinct personal existence; that he is, in truth, the Mighty God, existing from eternity, anterior to both individual men and the visible worlds, and the efficacious cause through which both man and the universe exist. We will adduce, six or eight pages farther on, some of the reasons brought forward by the Kabbalah to sustain its singular statement, that God, as Creator, assumes the form of *a man.* The Kabbalah differs, in almost every respect, from the modern theory of Positivism; but the kabbalists resemble a portion of the positivists in one particular, inasmuch as they set forth their doctrine as "the Religion of Humanity."

According to the Kabbalah, God is known by his names only. Each one of the Hebrew names of God is a special revealed aspect of the Nameless One. Of the Nameless One man knows nothing whatever, save the bare fact that he exists. [This kabbalistic truth has been recently and quite independently rediscovered by Mr. Herbert Spencer, who has published it to the world in the beginning of his book of "First Principles."] The Scriptures are explicit in affirming that "no man can see God, and live." Zophar, one of Job's comforters, inquires, "Canst thou by searching find out God?" St. Paul says of the Supreme, that he dwells in light unapproachable; and that no eye hath seen him, or can see him. John the Baptist testifies, saying, "No man hath seen God at any time: the only-begotten Son, who is in the bosom of the Father, he hath declared him."

The Nameless One is called, in the Kabbalah, אין סוף (*Æn-Soph*), the Limitless, or Name no name. For that which is known and named, is known and named, not from its substance, but from its limitations; and scientific men correctly aver, that whatsoever is unlimited, undefined, unclassifiable, is necessarily outside of natural science. Among the names of God which are known to men the most occult is אהיה (*Æhieh*, I AM), the Ancient of days, called by the kabbalists כתר (*Kether*, the Crown): this is the first sephirah, numeration, or revealed aspect of God. The next in order is designated by the kabbalists as חכמא (*Chokmah*, Wisdom), the Firstborn of the Ancient of days, and identified by the kabbalists with the ideal or principiating MAN, the Adam who is above: this is the second sephirah. The third sephirah is בינה *(Binah,* Understanding), which may be identified with the Greek Logos. Chokmah is masculine: Binah is feminine.

It is written in the Zohar,

> And the Lord said (*Gen.* vi. 7), "I will destroy man whom I have created from the face of the earth; both man and beast, and the creeping thing, and the fowls," &c. Here a distinction is made between the man who is of the earth, and the man who is above; for the earthly man is not alone indicated in this place, since the earthly

man without the heavenly man cannot be. For, without חכמא (*Chokma,* WISDOM, the man who is above, the authentic Adam), all things would be occulted. . . . If this אדם (*Adam*) should not exist, there would be no world. . . . This Wisdom that is hidden (this true Adam) institutes and corroborates the form of man, that man may be established in his own place. . . . This true Adam is the inward form, the spirit. . . . And in this inward form, which is seated on the throne, the perfection of all things appears. As it is written (*Ezek.* i. 26), "Above the heads of the Living Creatures was the likeness of a throne, . . . and on the throne—the appearance of a man," &c. It is also written (*Dan.* vii. 13), "I saw, in the night, visions, and, behold, one like unto the Son of man came with the clouds of heaven, and came unto the Ancient of days. . . . And there was given to him dominion and glory, and a kingdom. . . . His dominion is an everlasting dominion that shall never pass away, and his kingdom that which shall not be destroyed."— *Id. Rab.,* § 1119 to § 1130.

MAN, THE FORM OF ALL THINGS

Some men ask, "How can the chasm which separates between perception and the object of perception be bridged over? How can it be made certain, for instance, when men feel and see a tree, that there is a real tree in nature answering to the impressions made upon the senses?" Other men reply to them by asking, "How will you bridge over a chasm that never existed?" Perception is *an act of life*, containing in itself, synthetically, the perceiver and the thing perceived. When a man perceives a tree, he perceives that he perceives it; and, when he perceives that he is perceiving, he distinguishes between the perceiving subject and the object perceived, but without separating them. The subject and object of perception are weighed over against each other, and synthetically married, in the Kabbalistic Balance; and, when they are taken out of the Balance, the perception ceases to exist.

Outward objects make pictures of themselves on the retina of the eye: but no living subject was ever conscious of any picture on the retina of his own eye; and no living man ever passed, by induction, from the conscious perception of such a picture in his own eye to the affirmation of the outward existence that produced it. If there is no direct communication between the soul and the world, between spirit and matter, perception is impossible. If the soul cannot directly perceive an outward object because the soul is spiritual and the object is material, then the soul cannot (as, in fact, it does not) perceive the picture on the retina of the eye; for that also is material. Neither can the soul perceive a picture of the picture; for that, in like manner, is afflicted with the taint of matter. The same may be said of a picture of a picture of the picture; and so on to infinity. There is no chasm to be bridged. Perception is direct; and the supposed chasm, if any be supposed, is a mere nothing gratuitously created by the imagination.

What is matter? It is that which affects the senses. It is that which men see, hear, taste, smell, and feel. But to affect the senses is to act: even to affect the sense of touch by mere resistance is to act; for resistance is action. Who knows any thing about the mysterious transcendental *substance* that is said to underlie all the activities of matter? If it exist at all, it exists not for man; or, at the least, it exists not for man's senses; for (being by its nature inert) it produces no impression upon the senses: it exists, therefore, to man, as a mere abstraction cognizable by the mind. Matter is revealed by its activities only; and, to man, it is *force*. What is spirit? Spirit is revealed by its activities only: it is *force*. Matter and spirit are both of them forces. There is no reason why the two should not meet directly, in conjunction; and they do so meet. Every act of sensation shows a direct conjunction of matter and spirit.

Man is the Kabbalistic Balance. The human body is the theatre in which the conjunction and synthesis of the activities of the soul, with the activities of external nature, take effect. When a man feels any thing with the ends of his fingers, does he feel the feeling, or the feeling of the feeling, or the feeling of the feeling of the feeling? or does he feel the thing? He feels the thing.

Things not related to other things exist potentially only. When they come forth from potentiality, they do so by entering into relations. No isolated thing exists actually, or can so exist. The interdependence of existing things upon each other is called their *solidarity*. All things exist in solidarity; not otherwise. Things maybe transmuted in solidarity—coal may take the form of ashes and gas, water that of ice or of steam, sugar that of alcohol and residue, and so on—or material things may subsist, for a time, in a state of abeyance; but if any portion of matter, however inconsiderable, should be literally annihilated, the whole universe would at once collapse back into the aboriginal, doubly-occulted invisible Abyss of potentiality in potentiality (*thohu va bohu*). All things subsist in ever-changing relations to each other, and not otherwise.

Man is so related to the universe, and the universe is so related to man, that the two are aspects and conditions of each other. Neither can exist without the other. That kabbalistic form of man which is also the form of the universe is nothing other than the adaptation of the universe to the existence of man, and of man to the existence of the universe.

It is the doctrine of the Kabbalah, that the universe first[14] existed in the condition of potentiality in potentiality, afterwards in that of simple potentiality; and that the worlds were brought forth, finally, out of potentiality into actuality in the bond of solidarity, by the appearance, in actuality, of Adam, Humanity, the Collective Man. It is for this reason that the Adam from above is frequently characterized as the Maker of the worlds, or as he *by whom* the heavens and the earth are created. It is written in the Zohar,

> Before the Ancient of days had assumed his form, nothing was framed that was then to be framed; and all the worlds were void (existed potentially only).—*Id. Rab.*, 518.

---

[14] Logically *first*, not chronologically; for the evolutions here spoken of take place outside of time.

Before the Elder of elders assumed his form, he sculptured the Kings, arranged the Kings, and gave proportions to the Kings; *but they subsisted not.* And this is signified in the words (*Gen.* xxxvi. 32), "These are the kings that reigned in the land of Edom before there reigned any king over the children of Israel." In the land of Edom; that is, in the place which consists wholly in rigor."—*Id. Rab.*, 513, 514.

Why were the ancient worlds unable to subsist? Because man was not yet made. The constitution of man contains all things in its form; and, in accordance with man's form, all things may be disposed and distributed.—*Id. Rab.*, § 523, § 524. It is written (*Ezek.* i. 26), "And above the firmament that was over the heads of the Living Creatures was the likeness of a throne, as the appearance of a sapphire-stone; and over the likeness of the throne was the likeness as the appearance of a MAN upon it." As the appearance of a man, because man includes all forms. As the appearance of a man, because man includes all names. As the appearance of a man, because man includes all mysteries that were spoken and set forth before the creation of those first worlds which subsisted not.—*Id. Rab.*, § 511, § 512.

These kings that reigned in the land of Edom, the place where all rigor is found, were of feminine constitution.—*Id. Rab.*, 984. And they did not persist: they were not utterly abolished; but they did not persist; for they were from that part where all is feminine, and wherein there is no masculinity at all.—*Id. Rab.*, 991.

Outside of the constitution of man, nothing subsists. The ancient worlds were not abolished, but were removed out of their own forms until the form of Adam should appear.—*Id. Rab.*, 525, 526. When Adam was made, the ancient worlds were called forth again, but under other names; and were brought into a permanent state through those new names; so that they now appear in their place, but with names other than they had at first.—*Id. Rab.*, 531.

Before the worlds were made, face answered not to face: and therefore the first worlds were void and waste; for the first worlds were destitute of form. Those worlds appeared, shone, and were extinguished; as, when the red-hot iron on the blacksmith's anvil is smitten with the hammer, sparks blaze forth on every side, shine for an instant, and then go out. They were destroyed, and went out, because the Most Holy Elder had not produced forms, and because the workman was not yet at his work.—*Id. Rab.*, § 420 to § 424. Afterwards the workman applied himself to his work, assuming form.—*Id. Rab.*, § 427. Ancient is the habitation of the Elder of elders; and he sits on the throne of the sparks that he may subjugate them.—*Id. Rab.*, § 40.

It is obvious from the context that these kings of Edom are nothing other than arbitrary kabbalistic signs, or enigmatic symbols, denoting the worlds that were first made, but which subsisted not. Elsewhere, the Zohar speaks, much to the same effect, as follows, of these kings of Edom:

Before the Elder of elders, the most hidden of hidden things, instituted the forms of the Kings, and of the diadems of diadems, there was neither beginning nor ending. The Elder of elders, therefore, excavated, and instituted proportions in himself, and spread before himself a veil; and in that veil he sculptured and distributed the kings in their due proportions; but they did not subsist. And this is what is written (*Gen.* xxxvi. 29): "These are the kings that reigned in the land of Edom,'" &c. And the names were called of all those kings that were sculptured; but not one of them subsisted.—*Id. Rab.*, § 30 to § 33.

Thus far, the writers of the Zohar have spoken of the influence of the Collective Adam in establishing and maintaining the constitution of the universe. It would appear from other passages that they attribute no mean importance to the influence of individual men and women in sustaining or changing the order of nature. We quote one of these passages:

> R. Simon said to the companions, When that veil was expanded which you saw above us, I beheld all forms appearing in it, and shining in their places. —*Id. Rab.*, § 494. I see those forms shining now above it, waiting for the words of our mouths, that they may be crowned, and each one taken to its place; and, as they are explained by our mouths, they come forward, and are crowned, and are disposed in the order determined by our speech.—*Id. Rab.*, § 501. Blessed are ye in the world to come; for all the words that have come out of your mouths are holy and true, neither declining to the right hand nor to the left.—*Id. Rab.*, § 504.

This last passage bears upon the kabbalistic theory of magic. To persons ignorant of the fact of universal solidarity, and who deny the immediate contact of spirit with matter, magical changes in the order of society, or in that of the universe, seem, from the very nature of the case, to be impossible. The Mekubbalim have always, nevertheless, justly or unjustly, had the reputation of being magicians and miracle-workers. In magical processes, man first realizes changes in his own body, especially changes in his nervous system; and then through his body, which is itself a part of nature, he affects the order either of human society or of the material universe. But, in the solidarity of nature, action and re-action are equal. Man is, therefore, himself the straining and groaning fulcrum whereon he rests his own lever when he exerts magic power. He loses in effort, suffering, or humiliation, all that he gains in supremacy. In realizing the practical fruit of his exertions, he pays for it precisely all that it is materially worth to him. It appears, therefore, that men who work magically are induced to do so by motives of scientific curiosity, of disinterested benevolence, or of wanton and deep-seated malignity, not self-interest. It is reported that such of the kabbalists as have had the reputation of working miracles have all of them died suddenly, and nearly all of them violent deaths. Every exertion of human activity, outside the normal channels of old-fashioned labor, breeds violent and dangerous re-actions. We entertain the suspicion that honest labor is the only genuine magic.

The problem of remunerative labor—which involves the exceptional and world-famous problem of man's will and efficacy, and, consequently, the problems of his freedom, and of his possible merit and demerit, to say nothing of the contradictions inherent in the nature of property (which is a product of labor)—is essentially kabbalistic. It is a special sub-section of the general theory of magic.

It is not difficult to justify the methods of the Kabbalah from the standpoint of modern physical science. According to the scientific men, a thing is *known* when it has been compared with certain other things, distinguished from certain others, and classed as of this or that order. An object is said to be little known when it has little in common with things of which experience has been had, and well known when it has much, &c. A thing is said to be completely known when its community with other things is recognized as complete, and completely unknown when there is no recognized community at all. The scientific method consists of observation, comparison, induction, verification by experiment, &c. But observations and experiments are acts that take place in time; and, between such acts, intervals frequently occur. Induction is built up from a comparison of the results of observations or of experiments, or both; and such comparison involves an exercise of the memory. Now, upon what solid ground does the scientific man base his confidence in his own mental processes? For example, how does he know that events suggested to him by his memory really occurred? If the human mind testify of herself, her testimony is not valid. The scientific man, obviously, bases his scientific truth and certainty upon principles of whose validity he has no scientific certainty whatever. To that extent, therefore, he is entirely afloat.

The scientific man escapes this difficulty by saying that his knowledge is human knowledge, not absolute knowledge; that he accepts his natural faculties for better or worse, studying the laws of their action, and guarding himself, to the best of his ability, against error. He affirms that his postulates and conclusions are true, provided the human faculties he possesses, and the natural processes of reasoning, are trustworthy; not otherwise.

The real method of the Kabbalah is identical with the method of modern science. The object investigated by modern science is the world of nature; while that investigated by the kabbalistic philosophy is, primarily, the spiritual world, and afterwards the material world as dependent upon, and affected by, the spiritual world. The *objects investigated* differ: the *method of investigation is* the same.

The Kabbalah implicitly affirms, as postulates, a conviction of man's existence as a sentient and thinking being; a confidence in the evidence of the senses as verified by the understanding; a conviction that every event must have a cause, and a cause adequate to the effect; and, finally, a confidence in the uniformity of the operations of spirit and matter, or that the same cause, acting in the same circumstances, will always produce the same effect.

The Kabbalah claims to be that spontaneous philosophy which man, *quoad* man, naturally affirms now, always has affirmed, and always will affirm so long as man is man. The worlds affirmed by the Kabbalah are worlds known to man—worlds upon which man has set the seal of his own nature—worlds related to man, and of which man is the authentic form. Spinoza says there are an infinite number of worlds, and that two only of them all are known to man—the world of space, and the world of thought. Spinoza is more knowing than the Kabbalah; for the Kabbalah knows nothing of things whereof man is naturally ignorant. There is nothing in the Kabbalah that is not given in the nature of man.

The Kabbalah affirms implicitly, as a postulate, that every event must have an adequate cause; and that the same cause, acting in the like circumstances, always produces like effects. In so affirming, the Kabbalah affirms the reality of the fact of causation. The Kabbalah also asserts, by implication, that, naturally admitting the fact of causation, the human mind instinctively affirms the existence of God as Creator of the heavens and the earth. God as Creator, is, according to the Kabbalah, God in one of his names, and that not his highest name. This name (*the Creator*) is anthropomorphic. Man can conceive of God as he existed without the worlds, before the creation: he thus forms a conception of God as the Ancient of days, as the Elder of elders—a name higher than that of God as Creator of the world. The name *Æhieh*, I AM, the Elder of elders, which is the highest given among men, is still anthropomorphic. If man, by the process of abstraction, take away all elements of human form from his conception of the Ancient of days, his thought falls back upon that *real* Nothing which is the Nameless One—*Æn-Soph*. When man, in meditating upon God, soars above God's names, his thought becomes lost; for he meditates upon that which is, but exists not. Man knows nothing, and can conceive of nothing, that is absolutely outside of his own form.

Man was created in the image of God; not in the image of the Nameless One, however, who has no image, but in the image of God as known by his names. We read in the Zohar,

> Man subsists through that which is analogous to himself, and not otherwise. But what is analogous to man? The Holy Name. Therefore it is written (*Gen.* ii. 7), "Jehovah Elohim created man." Man was created in the full name, which is Jehovah Elohim, and analogous to man.—*Id. Rab.*, § 794, § 795. Man, therefore, is the form that comprehends all things.—*Id. Rab.*, § 799.

The name of God, as Creator of the universe, is, according to the Kabbalah, as we have already had occasion to remark, *Chokmah*, Wisdom. *Chokmah* is the second sephirah. The kabbalistic conception of Wisdom, the Creator of the worlds, working, as the second sephirah, in subordination to the Ancient of days, is supposed to have originated in the following passages of Scripture:

The Lord by Wisdom hath founded the earth;
By Understanding hath he established the heavens.
—*Prov.* iii. 19.

The Lord possessed me (Wisdom) in the beginning of
    his way,
Before his works of old.
From eternity was I anointed
From the beginning,
Before the earth was.
While the Abyss (*Heb. Thehom*) was not, was I
    brought forth;
While the fountains, heavy with waters, were not as yet.
Before the mountains were settled,
Before the hills, was I brought forth;
While as yet he had not made the earth,
Nor the open places, nor the fruitful soil.
When he established the heavens, I was there;
When he set a circle on the face of the deep;
When he spread the clouds above;
When he strengthened the fountains of the Abyss;
When he gave his decree to the sea,
That the waters should not pass his commandment;
When he laid the foundation of the earth—
Then was I by him as one brought up with him;
And I was his delight day by day,
Rejoicing always before him,
Rejoicing in the perfection of his earth;
And my delights were with the children of men.
—*Prov.* viii. 22–31.

Now, since God does all things wisely, and since Wisdom is always the same, God's method in creation never substantially varies. What men call the unvarying laws of nature, are, in reality, nothing in themselves; for they are mere aspects of God's unvarying manner of action. The sum of these laws, of these persisting aspects of the divine action, is the Greek Logos; but this sum is not at all the

Hebrew Word, or Wisdom. Wisdom is before its own effects, and before the unvarying aspects of its own operations. The Hebrew Word is God himself, as that spontaneous Divine Wisdom, as that Heavenly Man, that Creator of the heavens and the earth, of whose personal workings the impersonal Greek Logos is the ideal resultant and record only.

Force and Law are two different things. The Force of gravitation, for instance, is the mysterious efficacy by which material things naturally approach each other. The Law of gravitation, on the other hand, is this: "The force of gravitation acts always with intensities inversely proportional to the distances which separate gravitating bodies." Law determines forms, recurrences of phenomena, and the nature of evolutions. Every thing thrives, if it thrive at all, in obedience to the law of its kind. Lily-plants never become transfigured into those that bear roses, or into those that bear violets; and neither the seeds of the rose, nor those of the violet, ever give birth to lily-plants. The twig of a plum-tree grafted into a peach-tree is fed by the same soil, air, light, and moisture, which feeds the peach-twigs that surround it; but the twig of the plum-tree will always remain true to the law of its kind, will triumph over the necessities of its mere situation, and will always bear plums, just as it would have done if it had remained in its parent tree. The bark, fibers, leaves, fruit, of the plum-twig, are always the bark, fibers, leaves, fruit, of the plum-tree, and never those of the peach-tree.

The Hebrew Word is Force. The Greek Word is Law. The Greek philosophers never suspected their Eternal Logos of possessing personality, and of being *a man*. The Hebrew Word is *a heavenly* man—Adam Kadmon. The attempt to interpret Hebrew mysteries in the light of Greek philosophy has never brought forth any thing other than either nullity or confusion. In matters of high theology, Israel and Javan never understand each other.

The Christian religion, Hamitic-Shemitic in its origin, but generally rejected by the Shemites and Hamites, has become almost exclusively Aryan by adaptation, radical transformation, and adoption. The typical Aryan-Christians—the ultra-Protestants—receive their religion at second-hand; but they receive it defectively, since they receive with it neither the key of prophecy, nor the wand of miracles. Many of the original dogmas of Christianity, dogmas akin to those of the Kabbalah, have dropped out of modern theology; and dogmas alien to the primitive system have been added. It is matter for surprise that Aryan-Christians, living by a borrowed religion—a religion whose most essential mysteries are inexplicable from the Aryan standpoint—should see their way clear, as they do see it, to taunt the Shemites and Hamites with alleged intellectual, moral, and spiritual inferiority.

The Christian religion was, when it was first preached, foolishness to the Greeks, and to the Jews a stumbling-block. The Greeks laughed when they first heard of it. The possibility that the Word should "become flesh" was not in the conditions of their theory. To say that the Eternal Logos had become flesh, was, in the opinion of the philosophers, like saying that the intrinsic nature of the circle had suddenly assumed the form of a square. Christianity presented itself to the cultivated Greek mind, not as a stumbling-block, but as sheer absurdity. With the Jews the case was different. To men like Saul of Tarsus, thoroughly instructed in the occult theology of the Hebrews, Christianity was not foolishness, but, on the contrary, something full of danger to the Jewish state and religion. The new Christian doctrine, from the standpoint of the occult theology, was perfectly logical and consistent. There was no defect whatever in the theory. *All turned upon a question of historical fact to be determined by evidence.* The Jews said, *"Is it true that Jesus was really an incarnation, of the Celestial Wisdom, of the Maker of the worlds, of the Man who is above?"* Christians of the school of St. Paul answered by affirming the resurrection of Jesus from the dead, and his visible ascension into heaven in the presence of then surviving witnesses.[15] The apostle Paul says,

---

[15] This answer, though very convincing, is, after all, not precisely to the point. The fact that Jesus rose from the dead does not suffice to prove, of itself alone, the fact of his pre-existence in eternity, as the Maker of the worlds.

> Christ was buried, and rose again the third day according
> to the scriptures; and was seen of Cephas, then of the
> twelve: after that, he was seen of above five hundred
> brethren at once; *of whom the greater part remain unto*
> *this present*, but some are fallen asleep. After that, he
> was seen of James; then of all the apostles. And, last of
> all, he was seen of me also, as of one born out of due
> time[16]. . . . If Christ be not risen, then is our preaching
> vain, and your faith is also vain. Yea, and we are found
> false witnesses of God; because we have testified of God
> that he raised up Christ.—I *Cor.* xv. 4–15.

It was with no reminiscence of the Greek doctrine of the Word
which he had learned at Tarsus, but in the distinct apprehension of
a doctrine far more profound—the occult Hebrew doctrine of the
Word—that Paul said (I *Cor.* xv. 47), "The first man is of the earth,
earthy: the second man is the Lord from heaven." It was in the same
high presence that he said, respecting the Lord from heaven,

> He is the image of the invisible God, the First-born
> of every creature. For by him were all things created
> that are in heaven, and that are in earth, visible and
> invisible, whether they be thrones, or dominions, or
> principalities, or powers: all things were created by him
> and for him and he is before all things, and by him all
> things consist.—*Coloss.* i. 15–17.

This enumeration of thrones, dominions, principalities, and
powers, and the other salient points of the phraseology, are, all of
them, in the highest degree kabbalistic. Perhaps the passage is a
lost fragment of the Kabbalah, quoted by the apostle, but with an
incidental interpretation from his own point of view.

---

[16] Paul had his theological training under Gamaliel, and under the Mekubbalim.
He never saw Jesus in the flesh, but saw him in a vision, on the way to Damascus,
after the resurrection. He was never subjected, as the other apostles had been, to the
human influences of the Grand-Master of the Ideal.

That a man should be raised up who could write as St. Paul wrote is conceivable; but that he should have found communities, scattered all over the Roman empire, ready to receive his letters, and competent to read them understandingly and to fairly appreciate them, is matter for surprise. The fact of his letters being so received and appreciated would appear to prove that the characteristic occult doctrines of the Hebrew theology were widely spread among adepts at the time the apostle wrote.

The great schism in the early Church occurred while Paul was still living. Important elements of the kabbalistic doctrine passed, with Paul's interpretation and application of them, into the Apostolic Church of the Gentiles. Many of the Mekubbalim refused, however, to accept Paul's statement that Jesus is the Christ, the incarnation of the Word. The Kabbalah refused to abdicate in the presence of the new religion. The Jewish tradition, but in its most moderate form, became the inspiration of the Ebionitic Christians; and the Greek doctrines, associated with other Aryan doctrines from Persia and India, furnished occasion for the rise of the more noted heretical sects.

When the Greek theologians gave Japhetic expression to the original Shemitic-Hamitic dogmas of Christianity, which they did in their discourses, and by means of translations from Syriac into Greek, they unwittingly falsified the system. When they said and wrote that the Son (the Hebrew *Chokmah)* was made flesh, they tacitly meant to say, and were understood to say, that the Greek *Logos* (the Hebrew *Binah,* the impersonal Daughter) was made flesh.[17] This misapprehension created, from the beginning, a disastrous confusion in Christian theology, of which the effects are distinctly visible at the present day.

---

[17] *Chokma* is Son in respect to the Elder of elders, and Father in respect to individual men and women: in like manner, Binah (Understanding) is Daughter in respect to the Elder of elders, and Mother in respect to, &c. The Zohar says, "Thou shalt call Wisdom thy Father, and Understanding thy Mother." And again: "Wisdom is the Father; Understanding is the Mother: and these two are weighed in one Balance, as male and female."

In the Catholic theology, which, upon the whole, has remained logical and consistent, *Binah* has become embodied in the Blessed Virgin full of grace, whose personality is exclusively human. The Catholic Church departs from the early faith, if it depart from it at all, by excess, and not by defect. The Catholic Church teaches all that there is in Christianity. It is not for us to say that it teaches nothing more.

It has become our fixed conviction, from reflection on the inhering nature of the case, from a careful examination of the opinions expressed by the different writers of the New Testament, and from listening to expositions of the authentic doctrines of the Church, that Paul's theories are radically and disastrously defective. The general system which flows from the theory of divine evolutions, and from the affirmation that the personality of the second sephirah is the personality of Jesus, is a half-interpretation of Christianity, and is not at all adequate to the moral and practical purposes of a sufficient creed. Paul's system (defective in morality, and in internal evidence of its own truth, rather than in the matter of mere logic) is the system usually adopted by Christians affecting utter and unreasoning orthodoxy, and who receive, as such, their belief without rational investigation. The main practical difficulties of Paul's system are these: It is usually held unintelligently by its advocates; it is easily learned by its opponents, who often take its advocates by the flank, and in very unexpected occurrences; it teaches justification by faith without works, that is to say, it makes a substitution of arbitrary justification by the covering-over and non-counting of sin, in the stead of sanctification through amendment of life and the remission of sinfulness; it presents every particular conversion as a special miracle; it presents every supposable fact of damnation as having its cause and origin in the foreknowledge and predeterminate counsel of God; it presents the at-one-ment as consisting, on the one side, in the punishment of the innocent, which is an outrage on the moral sentiments, and, on the other side, in the counting of scoundrels as though they were honest men, which is another outrage; it confounds man's reason, by creating an issue between God's word in nature and God's word in scripture; it presents God as the voluntary author of sin; it naturally awakens hostility to

Christianity by calling God's justice in question; and it makes atheists among the unconverted. In it, as an exposition of the principles of Christianity by the Kabbalah, the Kabbalah spoils Christianity, and Christianity spoils the Kabbalah.

The Pauline doctrine against that of the early Gnostics, and the converse; the doctrine of St. Augustin against Manichæism, and the converse; Calvinism against Socinianism, and the converse—are three forms of one and the same contradiction-pregnant. The same motive—the alleged impossibility of a direct and immediate intercourse, union, and welding of spirit with matter, and of the infinite with the finite—which induced the Gnostics and the Manichæans to deny Christ's humanity, induces, to-day, the Socinians to deny his divinity. Calvinism refutes Socinianism, and, at the same time, calls it into being, and consolidates it: Socinianism refutes Calvinism; and yet, without Calvinism, Socinianism would have no reason for existing. Calvinism is the masculine term of this kabbalistic couple, and Socinianism is the feminine term. The lofty but peculiar metaphysical doctrine which is expounded in the Gospel of St. John, and in neither of the other Gospels, is the synthetic resolution of the contradiction-pregnant presented by the problem of the personality of Jesus.

It seems to be generally assumed by readers of the New Testament, that the sublime parts of St. John's Gospel are addressed exclusively to the religious sentiment. This is an error. The most transcendently spiritual passages of St. John's Gospel are precisely the parts of the New Testament which are the most intelligible. This error, and the ordinary natural instinctive antipathy of spiritually-minded persons to pure metaphysics, have conspired to cause the doctrine of St. John's Gospel to remain occult in the Church.

The doctrine of the Kabbalah and that of the New Testament are neither hostile to each other, nor yet the same. If it be deemed requisite to find the effectual point of contact of the two, we must look for it, not where the school of St. Paul places it, but in the theory of the Kabbaliatic Balance. The school of St. John, subsequent both logically and chronologically to that of St. Paul, corrects and completes the doctrine of St. Paul. The theory of LIFE, as it is expounded by the school of St. John, is the transfiguration of the kabbalistic theory of the Balance. St. John's doctrine carries "its witness in itself;" for the relations of its parts are perfectly logical, and the essential facts on which it is based may be verified, to every requisite extent, by each believer in his own private experience: "If any man will to do God's will, he shall know of the doctrine, whether it be of God."—*John* vii. 17.

There is nothing new in the morality taught by Jesus. Men were aware of the fact, before Jesus came, that God is the universal Father. David says (*Ps.* ciii. 13), "Like as a father pitieth his children, so Jehovah pitieth them that fear him." The following passages show plainly that Moses and the prophets recognized God as a Father:

> Do ye thus requite the Lord, O foolish people and unwise? is he not thy Father that hath owned thee? hath he not made thee and established thee?—*Deut.* xxxii. 6. Doubtless thou art our Father, though Abraham be ignorant of us: thou, O Lord! art our Father; our Redeemer from everlasting is thy name —*Isa.* lxiii. 16. But now, O Lord! thou art our Father: we are the clay, and thou our potter; and we all are the work of thy hand.—*Isa.* lxiv. 8. Have we not all one Father? hath not one God created us?—*Mal.* ii. 10. Zion said, The lord hath forsaken me, and my Lord hath forgotten me. Can a woman forget her sucking-child, that she should not have compassion on the son of her womb? Yea, they may forget; yet will I not forget thee.—*Isa.* xlix, 14, 15. As one whom his Mother comforteth, so shall Jehovah comfort you; and ye shall be comforted in Jerusalem.— *Isa.* lxvi. 13.

We know that it is written in the New Testament, "Ye have heard that it hath been said (in the law), Thou shalt love thy neighbor, and hate thine enemy." But Jesus never spoke those words. They are inexcusably calumnious.

Moses says (*Exod.* xxiii. 4, 5)—

> If thou meet thine enemy's ox or his ass going astray, thou
> shalt bring it back to him again; and if thou see the ass of
> him that hateth thee lying under his burthen, and wouldest
> forbear to help him, thou shalt surely help him.

Solomon says (*Prov.* xxv. 21, 22),

> If thine enemy be hungry, give him bread to eat; and,
> if he be thirsty, give him water to drink: for thou shalt
> heap coals of fire on his head (thou shalt cover him
> with burning shame), and the Lord will reward thee (by
> bringing him to repentance).

The following provisions of the Mosaic law were probably in the
mind of the writer of the above-quoted interpolated passage of the
New Testament; for we are convinced that the objectionable words
are an interpolation:

> Thou shalt not put forth to thy brother at *biting* (or
> interest)—*biting* of money, *biting* of victuals, *biting* of
> any thing which is susceptible of *biting*: to a foreigner
> thou shalt put forth at *biting*; but to thy brother thou
> shalt not put forth at *biting*.—*Deut.* xxiii. 19, 20.

The modern arbitrary distinctions between interest and usury
were unknown to Moses and the prophets. In their view, interest
and usury were the same thing. The one and the other were simply
that which, in the relation of borrowing and lending, "*biteth* like
a serpent." Moses did not believe in the utility of borrowed capital
on which interest is paid, or in the expediency of public debts which
mortgage a whole country to strangers.

David says (*Ps.* xv.),

> Lord, . . . who shall dwell in thy holy hill? . . . He that
> lendeth not out his money at *biting*!

The precept of "the Law" may be thus paraphrased:

> Unto foreigners thou shalt lend out thy money at usury;
> But thou shalt not take interest of thy brother:
> So shall the nations round about thee be mortgaged
> unto thee,
> And thou shalt not be mortgaged unto them;
> And thou shalt have dominion over them,
> And they shall not have dominion over thee.

The rich man, who, being in hell, saw Lazaras in Abraham's bosom, is supposed by the commentators—probably because no special offence is charged against him—to have been condemned to punishment for lending money to his brethren at *biting*, or interest. If the rich man and his relatives had listened effectually to Moses and the prophets, they would not have put out their money at interest to any but aliens from the commonwealth of Israel.

The difference between the new law, as it is now generally interpreted, and the old law, is this: The Christian, by the new law, may "bite" not only Jews and infidels, but also Christians; while, by the old law, Jew must never "bite" Jew.

We would like to ask the sentimentalists who accept all the moral teachings of Jesus, deny all the distinctive doctrines of Christianity, calumniate the Hebrew religion until they suppose they have driven it out of the memory of men, then assume distinctive Hebrew or Greek doctrines as their own,[18] and finally call themselves liberal "Christians," what they have in their religion that was not also in the religion of the prophet Isaiah, or else in that of Socrates and

---

[18] Mr. Jacob Norton, a man of very accurate erudition in matters of Hebrew and Masonic literature, has called the writer's attention to the fact, that the equivalent of the English expression, "O our Father!" occurs over and over again in the Hebrew text of the famous "eighteen prayers" that are regularly repeated three times every day by all pious Jews. Furthermore: the learned rabbi, Dr. A. Guinsburg, affirms that these same prayers were regularly recited in the synagogues, and probably in the temple of Jerusalem, long before the time of Christ. The venerable rabbi says he never heard either the antiquity or the authenticity of these prayers called in question, and asserts that it may easily be proved, if necessary, from genuine tradition, and from the internal evidences, that they are as old as he says they are.

Plato, centuries before the "Word became flesh." We shall probably be obliged to wait some time for an answer. If a man reject the theory of reminiscence, the doctrine of ideas, and the other characteristic teachings of Plato, why should he call himself a Platonist? If a man reject the peculiar features of Christianity which make it to be a special religion, apart from other religions, why should he call himself a Christian? There is no question here of personal moral character, or of the relative truthfulness of various creeds. If a man live by and profess a religion other than Christianity, he is no Christian, even if his religion prove to be better than Christianity. Nothing is ever gained, and often much is lost, in the long-run, by sentimental lying. The distinctive feature of Christianity is the fact—if it be a fact—that "the man Jesus is the Son of the living God WITH POWER: *two natures in one person.*"

As soon as the Pauline interpretation of Christianity had passed to the Aryan Gentiles, it gave occasion, in many places, for destructive heresies; and the most fatal of them all was the one which affirmed that Jesus was no real man, but a spiritual phantom only, a divine apparition, capable indeed of communicating God's will to man, but naturally incapable of dying on the cross. What is Christianity without the cross!

St. John, whose main work was subsequent to that of Paul, passed the whole latter part of his life in combating the heresy which denies that the "Son of God" is a real MAN. This heresy, which is the formal negation of Socinianism, is, obviously, the effectual equivalent of Socinianism, but in another sphere of ideas. St. John says,

> Many deceivers are entered into the world, who confess not that Jesus Christ is come *in the flesh.* This is a deceiver, and an Antichrist (2 *John* 7). Every spirit that confesseth not that Jesus Christ is come *in the flesh* is not of God. And this is that spirit of Antichrist, whereof ye have heard that it should come; and even now already is it in the world."—1 *John* iv. 3.

It is the denial of Christ's humanity, not the denial of his divinity, that is, in John's estimation, "Antichrist." To-day, it would seem that it is the denial of his divinity which is "a deceiver and an Antichrist."

We will now do our best to explain St. John's doctrine, first, in modern metaphysical language, without illustrations and comparisons; and then, afterwards, symbolically, in the express words which, according to John's Gospel, were spoken by the Master himself.

The act of consciousness is the typical act of life; for, the life of the consciousness, *or conscious life*, is the highest form of life known to man. The act of consciousness implies a subject and an object. Without the subject, there is no man, no soul, no life. Without the object, there is nothing upon which the soul may live. Life is the interpenetration and synthesis of activities proceeding from the external world on the one side, and of activities exerted by the soul itself on the other. It is the *Ego* that lives; but the life of the *Ego* is dependent upon, and on one side determined by, that in conjunction with which it lives. If the soul live in conjunction with the natural world, it will lead a natural and worldly life; the character of the life being determined, on one side, by the object. If the soul live in conjunction with the spiritual world, it will have its life, on one side, determined by the object, and the life will be spiritual. Now, men live in communion with other men. If, therefore, a man living a mere worldly life meet with a man who is living a spiritual life, the life of the second man may become the objective element of the life of the first man; and thus the first man may, through the life of the second man, begin to lead a spiritual life. The second man may convert the first one. Life is the synthesis of the subject and the object, of the soul and that which is not the soul, of that which is within and that which is without, of liberty and necessity.

Plato defines life to be self-originated motion of the soul, and therefore defines it inadequately—not altogether wrongly, but inadequately. He says in the Phædrus, "No one will fear to affirm that the power of self-motion forms the essence and the attribute of the soul; for that which receives motion from an exterior cause is not alive, while that which gives motion to itself is alive." Plato recognizes the principle of spontaneity, and ignores the principle of determination: he recognizes the principle of liberty, and ignores the principle of necessity.

Life is complex and synthetic. The interpenetration and synthesis of the activity of the soul with the activity of that which is not the soul, both activities meeting in the body, constitute the fact of life. Without the body, nature is without conjunction with the soul, and the soul without conjunction with nature; for the body is that special portion of external nature, in possible conjunction with all other portions of external nature, that is the counterpart of the soul in the Kabbalistic Balance.

The synthetic conjunction, in the body, of the activities of nature and of the soul, is LIFE.

The facts of our intellectual life, if known to us at all, are made known to us in consciousness; and those of our animal life are made known to us by direct observation. But the facts of our vegetative life are made known to us neither in consciousness nor by direct observation. A man eats consciously, but digests unconsciously. It is a matter of experience, that the vegetative life of the body is sustained by food. According to the theory spontaneously adopted by the great majority of mankind, food is the object, which, taken into the body, is assimilated to the body by the unconscious action of the soul, and made to be a part of the body. Without food, a man will die; and no food will sustain and nourish a body from which the soul is absent. Dead men neither eat nor digest. A few scientific men, it is true,—and, if we understand him rightly, Mr. Spencer is one of their number—deny that any spontaneous subject, any soul, really exists; but we are speaking of the common opinion. All reflecting persons may, perhaps, agree that the vegetative life of the body consists mainly and essentially in the assimilation of particles from the surrounding elements, and in the rendering back to the surrounding elements of particles that have formed a portion of the body.

It is lawful for a man, taking the popular opinion as it stands, to speak symbolically, and to say, "Truth is *the food* of the soul." It is also lawful for him to run the analogy out into its various ramifications, and to offer the circumstances of the vegetative life of man as illustrations of metaphysical truth. This is what Jesus—who, unlike some of the scientific men, teaches the real existence of the soul—actually does.

Jesus represents himself, in St. John's Gospel, as living a life apart from that of other men, and one superior to that of other men. He says that God, the Father, is the direct object of his life, and that his life is, therefore, divine-human: divine on the side of the object; and human on the side of the subject. He says—

> Not that any man hath *seen* the Father, save he which is of God: he hath *seen* the Father.—*John* vi. 46. I know him; for I am from him, and he hath sent me.—Ch. vii. 29.

If Jesus saw the Father, and knew him, and if no other man, before Jesus came, had ever seen the Father, or ever known him directly, it follows that the life of Jesus differed in kind from that of the persons to whom he addressed the words here quoted. He was *God-man* and *man-God,* not, as St. Paul would seem to intimate, by a transfusion of persons, but, on the contrary, by a *communion of* LIFE. John the Baptist says,

> No man hath seen God at any time: the only-begotten Son, which is in the bosom of the Father, he hath declared him.—*John* i. 18.

Jesus lived, according to the texts, on one side in the Father; but he lived also in communion with men. Men, therefore, by making the life of Jesus the objective element of their own lives, could themselves live, through him, in the Father. He says,

> As the *living* Father hath sent me, and I LIVE BY the Father; so he that EATETH ME, even he shall LIVE BY me.—*John* vi. 57. He that hath seen me hath seen the Father; and how sayest thou, then, Show us the Father? Believest thou not that *I am in the Father,* and *the Father in me?*—Ch. xiv. 9, 10.

Here the force of the symbol becomes manifest. It becomes still more manifest in the following passages:

> The *bread* of God is he which cometh down from heaven, and giveth life unto the world.—*John* vi. 33. I am the *bread of life*: he that cometh to me shall never hunger, and he that believeth on me shall never thirst.—Ch. vi 35. I am that *bread of life*.—Ch. vi. 48. I am the *living bread* which came down from heaven: if any man *eat of this bread* he shall *live* forever.—Ch. vi. 51.

It is useless to multiply passages. The key-word to John's Gospel is this very word LIFE. It is the doctrine of John's Gospel, that man is naturally mortal; that Jesus was naturally immortal because he "lived by the Father;" and that men obtain immortality by coming, through Christ, to a participation in the life of the Father. Jesus says,

> Ye will not come unto me that ye might have *life*.—*John* v. 40. He that believeth on the Son hath everlasting *life;* and he that believeth not the Son *shall not see life*.—Ch. iii 36. Except ye *eat of the flesh* of the Son of man, and *drink his blood*, ye have no *life* in you.—Ch. vi. 53. Whoso *eateth my flesh*, and *drinketh my blood*, hath *eternal life*; and I will raise him up at the last day.—Ver. 54. I am the resurrection and the *life*: he that believeth in me, though he were dead, yet shall he *live*; and whosoever *liveth* and believeth in me *shall never die*.—Ch. xi 25, 26. *Because I live*, ye shall *live* also. At that day ye shall know that I am in my Father, and ye in me, and I in you.—Ch. xiv. 19, 20.

The union of the Son with the Father consisted neither in an assumption on the part of the Son of the Father's person, nor yet in an incarnation of the Father's person in the Son: it consisted in *a communion of* LIFE.

["Pater omnipotens, æterne Deus: Qui cum unigenito Filio tuo et Spiritu Sancto, unus es Deus, unus es Dominus: *non in unius singularitate Personæ, sed in unius Trinitate substantiæ.*" What is *substance?* The word denotes an abstraction existing to the mind. *Substance* is *reality* of existence. As soon as the meaning of the word *substance* is rightly apprehended, the theory of the Divine Presence in the sacraments changes its aspect.]

Jesus was "one" with the Father in the same way that the disciples were "one" with each other, and "one" with him. He says,

> I pray that they all may be ONE; as thou, Father, art in me, and I in thee, that they also may be ONE in us: that the world may believe that thou hast sent me. And *the glory which thou gavest me I have given them; that they may be* ONE, even as we are ONE: I in them, and thou in me, that they may be made perfect in ONE.—*John* xvii. 21–28. Holy Father, keep through thine own name those whom thou hast given me, that they may be ONE, *as we are.*—Ver. 11. I and my Father are ONE.—Ch. x. 30. My Father is greater than I.—Ch. xiv. 28.

From the standpoint of John's Gospel, it is logically inevitable that death must mean death, and not an inferior life; and that life must mean life, and neither prosperity, nor any thing other than simply life. Moreover, damnation must mean simply absolute death, and not an eternal life of misery. When the soul that sinneth dies it ceases to live. It is written,

> He that heareth my word, and believeth on Him that sent me, hath everlasting life, and shall not come into damnation, but is passed from death unto life.—*John* v. 24. For God sent not his Son into the world to damn the world, but that the world through him might be saved. He that believeth on him is not damned; but he that believeth not is damned already, because he hath not believed in the name of the only-begotten Son of

God. And this is the damnation, that light is come into
the world, and men loved darkness rather than light,
because their deeds were evil.—Ch. iii. 17–19.

If we look at the visible Church of Christ as it now stands on the
rock, and endeavor to account for its existence by following up, in
the fatality of their relations, the chain of antecedents and consequents which connect it historically with its beginning, we come
to Jesus as the first link of the chain; for beyond him no antecedent belonging to the series can be pointed out. The visible Church,
the *cherubic form* of the spiritual Israel, the magical River of Life,
the terrestrial Eden, the Miracle of the Ages, *originated* eighteen
hundred years ago in the spontaneity of Jesus. The personality of
Jesus, ever-present in its operative energies, appears to us to-day, in
and through the visible Church, just as it did to the early disciples,
extrahuman and inexplicable.

What do we care to-day, any of us, for the learned remarks
that judicious critics may have to put forward respecting the
original intent and application of the Messianic prophecies? Is
it not competent to the spirit of *Adam Kadmon*, the spirit of
Humanity, the spirit that rules and interprets the ages, to inter-
polate, under the words of the prophets, meanings of which the
prophets never dreamed? When we hear poetry of like nature
and tenor with that which is quoted below chanted in church,
we believe every word of it (so long as the organ is playing),
just as the servant-maids and the coal-heavers who sit near us
believe it. When we go out of the church, and hear the noise
of the street, and believe no longer, are we any greater, nobler,
better, or even wiser, than we were while we were inside the
building, before the altar, and believing? It is written in the Old
Testament,

But thou, Beth-lehem Ephratah,
Though thou be little among the thousands of Judah,
Yet out of thee shall he come forth unto me
Who shall be ruler in Israel;

Whose goings-forth have been from of old—
From the days *of* eternity.—*Mic.* v. 2.

Jehovah himself shall give you a sign;
Behold, a virgin shall conceive,[19] and bear a son,
And shall call his name Immanuel.—*Isa.* vii. 14.

Unto us a child is born;
Unto us a son is given:
And the government shall be upon his shoulder:
And his name shall be called
Wonderful, Counsellor, the Mighty God,
The Everlasting Father, the Prince of Peace.—*Isa.* ix. 6.

THE SEPHIROTH—THE FIRST TRIAD

The ten sephiroth are the ten successive steps, or stages, by which, if we may believe the Kabbalah, the name of the Supreme becomes known to men. Each sephirah is a distinct special name and aspect of the Most High.

The Ancient of days (called also the Elder of elders) is the first Sephirah. The Ancient of days is known to the Mekubbalim by many titles. He is called Kether (the Crown); also the Orient (or the Beginning), the Cause of causes, Æhieh, Black Color, Bottomless Depth, the Fear of the Lord, Light Unapproachable, the Eternal, the White Head, and the like.

The existence of the Ancient of days (as himself) involves, by necessary contradistinction, the existence of that which is *not* himself. But, exclusively of the Ancient of days, *nothing* is. That NOTHING is uncreated; for it stands in the Kabbalistic Balance as the negation—the necessary correlative counterpart, by way of contradiction—of the Ancient of days. That *nothing* is the aboriginal Abyss. It is written, "The earth was without form, and void; and darkness was on the face of the Abyss."[20] From that Abyss all cre-

---

[19] Heb.: "Behold, the young woman hath conceived, and shall bear," &c.

[20] תהרם, *Thehom*, the Abyss.

ated things were drawn forth. The world is created out of *nothing.* In that aboriginal *nothing,* the eye of the Ancient of days saw, from the beginning, all things as existing potentially and without forms; even to creatures of whom it was already written, that they should one day array themselves against their Maker, defy his power, and be forgiven. For the Elder of elders "calleth things that are not as yet as though they actually were." The original *nothing* is the immanent substance of the existing worlds, the uncreated and persistent root of every thing that is *not* God. While the creatures exist potentially only, they are real, but not actual: it is not until they are brought forth into visibility, through being clothed with form, that they become both real and actual. Whether existing visibly or invisibly, the substance and ground of the creatures, as creatures, is *nothing.*

It is obvious, from the nature of the case, that the Abyss, the potential world, the original nothing, the possibility of things, must be uncreated. Why? For this reason. If God created the original possibility, that creation of the original possibility was itself *possible* with God; and a new possibility rises up behind the possibility first considered. This new possibility is a prior condition requisite to the very being of the possibility first considered. If we treat this new possibility (which we have found, on the hypothesis that the original possibility was *created,* to be prior to that *original* possibility itself)—if we treat this new possibility as we did the other, still another possibility will rise up behind this new possibility; and so on to infinity. If, therefore, the *original* possibility was created, that possibility was by no means original; for it must have been preceded by another possibility, and this last by another; and so on.

The possibility of a particular act of creation is a condition logically prior to the creative act itself; for, if the particular creation be impossible, it will never take place. The possibility is not made to be by the very fact of creation; for the particular creation would have remained possible although the actual creation had never taken place. The greater portion of the Abyss, the greater part of the possibilities of things, have, indeed, not yet been realized, and in all probability they never will be. The possibility of an act of creation is, therefore, a condition logically prior to and independent of that act itself; and this reasoning applies as well to the first act of creation as to any other. The possibility of creation, the universe in *potentia,* the Abyss, therefore, existed before the very first act of creation, and is itself *uncreated.*

This reasoning, though subtle, and apparently verbal, is supposed to be in reality accurate, logical, and conclusive.

The original *nothing* was, from the beginning, outside of the Elder of elders—opposite to him—other than himself. *In it the Elder of elders was reflected as in a mirror.* The image of the Elder of elders, eternally reflected in that *nothing* which was from the beginning, is the Microprosopus. The Elder of elders is the Macroprosopus. It is written in the Zohar,

> The parts of the Microprosopus (זעיר אפין *Zoir-Aphin,* the shorter face or aspect) are distributed and clothed according to the forms of the Most Holy Ancient of days, hidden in all things.—*Id. Rab.,* § 508. . . . These forms of the Microprosopus are, therefore, disposed according to the forms of the Macroprosopus (אריך אפין, *Arik-Aphin,* the greater face or aspect); and the forms of the Microprosopus are extended here and there in human figure and similitude, in order that the spirit hidden in all parts of it may be drawn forth.—*Id. Rab.,* § 510.
>
> The Elder of elders is called *Arik-Aphin* (long-face, or Macroprosopus); but he who is outside is called *Zoir-Aphin* (short-face, or Microprosopus); in contradistinction from the Silent Holy Elder, the Holiest of the holy (who has no face). And, when the Microprosopus looks back upon the Macroprosopus, all things in it are reduced to order, and its face is lengthened while it is looking; but its face is not always long like that of the Elder of elders.—*Id. Rab.,* § 54, 55. . . . There is no left-hand side to the occult Elder; for, with him, every thing is on the right," —*Id. Rab.,* § 81.

In the above figure, a representation is given of the kabbalistic "answering of face to face."[21] The superior face denotes that of the non-cognizable Head. "That which is below answers to that which is above." Above is the Macroprosopus; below, the Microprosopus. The picture denotes a special phase and moment of the Kabbalistic Balance.

It is written in the Zohar, "The Macroprosopus and the Microprosopus are so designated to contradistinguish (לקבליה, *le-kbl-ih*) them from the Silent Holy Elder, the Holiest of the holy (who has no name)." [*Le-*KBL: *according to the opposition; as contradistinguished from.*] The word *Kabbalah* has, therefore, an exoteric and an esoteric signification: used esoterically, it signifies that which is received by tradition; used esoterically, it signifies the weighing in the Balance, the doctrine of oppositions, of contradistinctions, of contradictions-pregnant.

---

[21] This picture may be found in Eliphaz Levi's "Dogma and Ritual of Transcendent Magic," and also in the published "Ritual" of some of the very high Masonic degrees.

The theory of the Kabbalah is the ancient theory of emanations, but transformed and idealized. It recognizes no material flux. The Kabbalah says expressly, "THOUGHT *is the source of all that is.*" The evolution of the universe is a process of thought, not a flow of matter. It is, in one aspect, a poem; in another, it is a logical argument. In every aspect, the universe is a work of art. Reality is adequate to thought; and volition, which is a form of thought, is equivalent to existence. It is written in the Zohar,

> The Holy Elder (the Macroprosopus) is non-manifest. The Microprosopus is either manifest or non-manifest: as manifest, it may be written with letters.—*Zeniutha,* ch. iv. § 1, 2. There are twenty-two occult letters, and twenty-two manifest letters; and the occult and manifest are weighed over against each other in the Balance.— *Zen.,* iv. § 10, 11. . . . (That which is above is male; that below, female:) as it is written, "The sons of God saw the daughters of men, that they were fair."—§ 16.
>
> R. Simon said, All things that I have spoken of the Holiest Elder, and all that I have spoken of the Microprosopus, all are the same, all are one; and there is no place here for separation. Blessed be He, and blessed be his Name, for ever and ever.—*Id. Sut.,* § 240. He and his Name are one.—*Id. Sut.,* § 354. This is the sum of the doctrine. The Elder of elders is in the Microprosopus. All was; all is; all shall be. Mutation is not, was not, and shall never be.—*Id. Rab.,* § 920.

From the Ancient of days, who is the first sephirah, nine other sephiroth proceed, making ten in all. "There are ten sephiroth, not nine of them only; ten, and not eleven." The procession, from the Ancient of days, of the nine sephiroth, is thus explained and illustrated in the Zohar:

> The Most Holy Ancient One (blessed be his name!) separates himself, and always more and more. In all

things he is separate, yet not fully separate: for all
things cohere in him; and he is in all things, and he is
all things. He possesses form, and yet he is as though he
were formless. He assumes form in order that he may
sustain all things; and yet he is without form, since he is
nowhere found. As possessing form, he produces NINE
LIGHTS, which shine from him out of the form he has;
and these lights shine from him, and emit flames, and are
spread abroad on all sides like rays scattered from a lofty
beacon-fire. If any one approaches these rays to examine
them severally, he finds nothing but the single beacon-
fire. So also it is with the Most Holy Ancient One. He is
that lofty beacon-fire which is hidden in all occultations.
He himself is found nowhere, save in those rays which
are spread abroad, revealed, and hidden. And these rays
are called the Holy Name; and, because of that Name, all
of them are one.—*Id. Sut.*, § 41 to § 47.

"Thought is the source of all that is." Thought is the first sephirah, the Ancient of days. Thought implies a subject which thinks,
and also an object thought. The thinker and the object thought are
weighed over against each other in the Kabbalistic Balance.

God is Intelligent-Cause. He is also self-sufficient; and, as such,
be creates himself eternally. As creator, he is the thinker; as created
by himself, he is himself the object thought. He is at once the subject and the object of his own thought. He is that which eternally
creates, that which is eternally created, and the eternal act of creation; that which eternally thinks, that which is eternally thought,
and the eternal act of thinking. His essence involves existence. He
is in eternity, and he exists eternally. The Kabbalah says, "The
Ancient of days (blessed be his name!) exists in three heads, which
are one head."

The Supreme, as thinking subject, is called, in the Kabbalah, Chokmah (Wisdom), and is regarded as male. As himself the object of his
own thought, he is called Binah (Understanding), and is regarded as
female. Binah is the Supreme as objective to himself. "Chokmah is

the Father; Binah is the Mother: Chokmah and Binah are weighed in one Balance as male and female." It is written in the Zohar,

> The Father and the Mother inhere in the Elder, and are his conformations.—*Id. Sut.*, § 393. The Father and Mother are produced from the Most Holy Elder, belong to him, and in him cohere. Through them the Microprosopus is produced from the Most Holy Elder, and is united with him.—§ 397, 398.

The first three sephiroth are the three constituent elements of the divine self-consciousness. The affirmation of the Supreme as existing in the form of the first triad of the sephiroth is an affirmation of the personality of God; for personality is an aspect of consciousness.

Before the evolution of Chokmah and Binah, the Supreme was devoid of self-consciousness (the form of man), and therefore of volition, which is a product of personal consciousness: consequently, the first worlds persisted not; for the persisting worlds are a product of God's volition. It is written, "In the beginning, God created *(bara,* bare) the heavens and the earth; and the earth was *thohu va bohu* (a contingent potentiality of existence, and in a potentiality of existence—an occultation that was occulted in still another); and darkness was on the face of the *Thehom* (the Abyss)." When the Supreme evolved himself into Trinity through becoming self-conscious (we speak here of logical, not chronological, sequence), the worlds passed from double into simple occultation; and the *Thehom* became a mere potentiality, and no longer a potentiality occulted in another potentiality. And herein is mystery.

A stream of water that should well forth in the *Thehom,* the Abyss, would spring from *nowhere,* and would flow *nowhere*: it would have no status in space; it would exist in the form of infinitely-attenuated spray, mist, or dew. If, however, on the contrary, that same water should well forth in the world of actuality, upon the earth, it would meet with obstacles, would wear for itself a channel, and would become a river, having a certain individuality of its own. So it is with the fact of personality. A person is a living-subject; but if that subject have no object, be weighed against nothing whatever in the Kabbalistic Balance, it will not be truly alive, and will be the mere potentiality of a person.

If it be a fountain of light, and not one of water, that streams forth into the *Thehom,* the result will be analogous: the light will illuminate nothing—for there is nothing in the *Thehom* to be illuminated—and the light itself will be and remain invisible.

Combining these two figures, we obtain a phrase that has been famous among the Mekubbalim—"The Dew of Lights."

> This is that manna which is provided for the just in the world to come. On this dew the heavenly saints are fed.—*Id. Rab.,* § 48, 49. By this dew the dead are raised up in the world to come.—§ 45.

The Dew of Lights is the potentiality of the Divine Subject, of the Divine Personality. This is that "Crystalline Dew" which is mentioned in the Zeniutha. It is written,

> The non-cognizable Head is framed and prepared (or is to be conceived) after the similitude of *a skull* [Kether] filled with *crystalline dew* [Chokmah]: the *covering membrane* [Binah] of this skull is transparent and closed.—*Zeniutha,* i. § 10.

Chokmah is called by many names; as the Word, Firstborn, Will, Jah, Amen, What? Thought, Eden, and the like.

Binah is, in like manner, called by many names; as Sister, Wonderful Light, River flowing out of Paradise, Daughter, the House of Wisdom, the Face of the Sun, the Fire consuming itself, and the like.

THE SEPHIROTH—THE SECOND TRIAD

The worlds were brought forth from potentiality into actuality through the volition of the Supreme. But what moved the Supreme (who is complete in himself, to whose perfection nothing is lacking), and induced him to create the worlds? Spontaneous pity moved him, and loving-kindness for the creatures he saw in the Abyss (the *Thehom*), where they were subsisting potentially only, and without any actuality at all.

Pity or mercy, חסד (*Chesed*), is the fourth sephirah. Sometimes this sephirah is known also as גדולה (*Gedulah*), greatness, magnificence, generosity. The fourth sephirah is called by many names as Water, White Fire, White Clothing, El, Abraham, Silver, Michael, the Lion's Face, and the like.

But pity, standing alone, is barren, is virtual only. Pity implies justice as its correlative opposite. Pity and justice, like wisdom and understanding, are weighed against each other in the Kabbalistic Balance as male and female. The actuality of the one implies the actuality of the other.

Justice, דין (*Din*), is the fifth sephirah. Sometimes this sephirah is known also as גבורה (*Gibborah*), rigor, severity. The fifth sephirah is called by many names; as Elohim, Isaac, Red Color, Red Fire, Gold, the Golden Altar, Gabriel, Metatron, the North, Judgment, Fear, Sanctification, Truth, Merit, and the like.

The synthesis of mercy and justice in the Kabbalistic Balance is BEAUTY. Beauty, תפארת (*Tiphareth*), is the sixth sephirah. This sephirah has many names; as Yellow and Green Colors, Sun, Rising Sun, Shaddai, High Priest, the World to Come, the Husband of the Church, Holy King, Terrible, and the like.

Woman is justice: man is mercy. Marriage, the synthetic union of the two, is *Tiphareth*—beauty; and marriage is always beautiful when the woman is just to the man, and the man is magnanimous to the woman. Woman is fatality: man is spontaneity, liberty. Fatality and liberty, the two aspects of human life, naturally contradict each other, deny each other, and exclude each other; but when liberty, as against fatality, takes the form of Magnanimity—the fourth sephirah—and fatality, as against liberty, takes the form of Justice—the fifth sephirah—then Beauty—the sixth sephirah—immediately comes into being as the sabbath of rest for the two.

It will be observed that the figure on the 69th page [originally on

p. 79 of the 1872 edition—*ed.*] is in the form of the Blazing Star. The points of the star are represented by the opposing crowns and by the angles of the elbows. The Cubical Stone and the Blazing Star are equivalent symbols: each face of the stone answers to a point of the star.

The two sephiroth, Mercy and Rigor, are denoted in the picture by the hair parted in the middle, and "hanging in equilibrium." Sometimes Beauty is denoted by the forehead, and sometimes by the beard. All the sephiroth are denoted in the Balance by parts and adjuncts of the Head only; for it is written,

> The scripture says, "Lord, revive thy work in the midst of the years." This is said of the Ancient of days. What is this "work"? Microprosopus.—*Id. Rab.*, § 738. But nothing is revealed of the Holy Elder save the head only; for he is the Head of all heads.—*Id. Sut.*, § 57.

We will quote some of the passages of the Zohar in which the sephiroth are spoken of as denoted by the lips, beard, forehead, and the like of the Macroprosopus:

> The beard hides not the lips, which are red and rosy. As it is written, "His lips are like roses."—*Cant.* v. 13. The lips mutter *Severity*; they mutter *Wisdom*. To them pertain good and evil, life and death.—*Id. Sut.*, § 678–680. In the book of dissertations of R. Jebha, the elder, it is affirmed and stated that the beard of the Macroprosopus begins at the supreme *Benignity*. And so it is written (I *Chron.* xxix. 11), "Thine, O Lord! is the greatness (*Gedulah*) and the power (*Gibborah*) and the beauty (*Tiphareth*)," &c. This affirmation is correct. These things are so, and thus begin.—*Id. Sut.*, § 663, 664. The forehead of the Macroprosopus is called Well-pleasedness.—*Id. Sut.*, § 87. When it is unveiled, loving-kindness is found in all worlds, and all prayers are accepted, and the face of the Microprosopus

is illuminated from above, and all things appear in mercy.—§ 90, 91. And all judgments are turned aside, and mercy is found in their stead.—§ 93. Also the Gehenna fire withdraws into its place, and sinners have a respite. —§ 94.

Certainly, so far as the Elder of elders, the White Head, discloses his forehead, great mercies are found everywhere; but, when that forehead is covered, the Microprosopus is clothed with unmitigated judgments, and, if it be lawful so to speak, mercy becomes judgment.—*Id. Rab.*, § 678–680. The forehead of the Microprosopus is the forehead of the visitation of sinners. When that forehead is uncovered, there is a rising-up of the judgments of the Lord against such as blush not for their evil works. This forehead is rosy-red; but it becomes as white as snow whenever the forehead of the Elder of elders is uncovered before it in the hour called the time of loving-kindness for all.—*Id. Sut.*, § 496–499. When the forehead of the Macroprosopus is unveiled, it quenches the fire of the forehead of the Microprosopus while this second forehead is inspecting the sins of the world that blushes not for its works. As it is written (*Jer.* ii. 3), "Thou hast an harlot's forehead, and refusest to be ashamed."—*Id. Rab.*, § 592, 593.

Pity, mercy, magnanimity, generosity—the fourth sephirah—is active, spontaneous, and free. Commiseration, a human passion which (because it is a passion) counts not among the sephiroth, is responsive and female, or subsists in instinctive re-action and communication, and therefore belongs to the order of fatality. Pity is distinctively human. Dumb animals sometimes commiserate each other; but no dumb animal ever yet experienced the sentiment of spontaneous pity.

Pity belongs to the soul; commiseration and compassion belong to the body. Pity is indefectible; but commiseration and compassion turn easily into jealousy, envy, and hatred. The same principle of instinctive sympathy which impels us to aid those who, through suffering, are more unhappy than we are, causes us to conspire against all superiority that imparts to others a happiness we do not possess. We never envy the trees for their tallness; but we envy the natural advantages of other men: this is because we live in sympathetic relations of action and re-action with men; while, between ourselves and the trees, no real social bond exists.

The soul and the body, the spiritual man and the animal man, liberty and fatality, are weighed over against each other in the Kabbalistic Balance. The apostle Paul says,

> The flesh lusteth against the spirit, and the spirit against the flesh; and these are contrary the one to the other.—*Gal.* v. 17. They that are according to the flesh do mind the things of the flesh; and they that are according to the spirit, the things of the spirit: for to be carnally-minded is death; but to be spiritually-minded is life and peace.—*Rom.* viii. 5, 6. I delight in the law of God after the inward man; but I see another law in my members warring against the law of my mind, and bringing me into captivity to the law of sin which is in my members.[22]—*Rom.* vii. 22, 23.

The first experience, by an individual man, of the sentiment of magnanimous mercy, is usually coincident with his first act of real and effectual self-consciousness; and it is through an act of consciousness that the war between the law of the mind and the law of the members is brought to an end, and replaced by peace. Pitiless men are men who have not yet outgrown the thraldom of mere animal existence; men who have, in fact, a certain consciousness, such as the animals have, but, as yet, know nothing of that spiritual

---

[22] St. Paul is very quick to discern a contradiction in the Balance; but he frequently fails to perceive the synthesis. It is for this reason that his writings, though powerful to produce conviction of sin, are less potent than those of St. John in effecting conversions.

consciousness of which we have spoken. The first experience of the sentiment of spontaneous pity marks a critical epoch in the history of individual men. It is the first round in the ladder of spiritual religion. St. Paul places charity—not alms-giving, but pity, mercy, generosity—above faith and hope. He says, "Though I bestow all my goods to feed the poor, and though I give my body to be burned, *and have not charity,* it profiteth me nothing." And again: "And now abideth faith, hope, charity, these three; but the greatest of these is charity." The day and the hour in which an individual man first knows the sentiment of true charity is always remembered. No man was ever born again (and no people was ever born again) without being consciously aware of the spiritual transformation, and without retaining a distinct recollection of the event.

THE SEPHIROTH—THE THIRD TRIAD

The first triad—thought, wisdom, understanding—is intellectual. The second triad—mercy, justice, beauty—is moral and spiritual. The third triad is physical, or dynamic.

The seventh sephirah, the first term of the physical or dynamic triad, is called not only נצח (*Netsech,* Victory), but also Jehovah Sabaoth, Eternity, Moses, JACHIN (or the name of the right-hand column in the porch of Solomon's temple), &c. Let us stop with Jachin. The word Jachin signifies "Force that establishes." Jachin is *energy.*

The eighth sephirah, the second term in the physical triad, or הוד (*Hod,* Glory), is also called Elohim Sabaoth, Aaron, King's Daughter, the Old Serpent, BOAZ (or the name of the left-hand column in the porch of Solomon'stemple), &c. Let us stop this time with Boaz. The word Boaz signifies "Strength of endurance." Boaz is *strength.*

Netsech and Hod, Victory and Glory, Jachin and Boaz, are energy and strength. The Kabbalah says,

> By Netsech and Hod (Victory and Glory) *force* is multiplied. All *powers* born in the universe flow from these two. They are called *the armies* of the Eternal.

We may illustrate the weighing of these two correlatives over against each other in the Kabbalistic Balance by instancing the natural working of any material machine; of a locomotive steam-engine, for example. If the steam be not utilized in the locomotive, but is allowed to disseminate itself in space, it will spread itself on every side, exert itself nowhere, and will fail to reveal itself as force. On the other hand, so long as the machine is unactuated by the steam, the materials of which it is composed will remain inert, and no motion will be originated. The true working-power of a locomotive steam-engine is a synthetic result, a joint product of the energy (*Jachin*) furnished by the steam, and of the resisting strength (*Boaz*) of the materials entering into the composition of the machine.

The ninth sephirah, יסוד (*Jesod*, Foundation), is the synthesis of Jachin and Boaz, of energy and strength: it is *working power.*[23]

The third triad, the physical or dynamic triad, is, therefore, energy, strength, working-power. The Kabbalah says (*Idra Rabba,* § 600), "The forehead of the Microprosopus is *Netsech* (Victory)." We suspect that Netsech and Hod, Jachin and Boaz, energy and strength, are denoted by the two eyes of the Microprosopus; but we have never yet been able to find the express passage of the Zohar that would confirm our suspicion. We do not fully understand the following extracts, but give them, nevertheless, in the hope that the reader may be able to make out their meaning:

> In the Microprosopus there is a right eye and a left eye; and these two are of diverse colors. But the eye of the

---

[23] The useful effect, or "working-power," of a machine, is the fraction that expresses the amount of work performed as compared with the power applied. The power applied is expressed by unity. Thus, if the machine perform two-thirds of the work applied to it, one-third of the power applied is lost by friction, and two-thirds is the useful effect of the machine.—*Baker's Mechanics.*

Macroprosopus is not at all on the left; for both eyes
are one eye, and both are on the right. For this reason,
they are not two eyes, but one eye. And this eye, which
is the eye of observations, is always open; but the eyes of
the Microprosopus are not always open, and they have
eyelids to protect them.—*Id. Rab.*, § 149–152.

The children of Israel said (*Exod.* xvii. 7), "Is
the Lord among us, or not?" This question makes
a distinction between the Microprosopus, who is
called Tetragrammaton (and is with men), and the
Macroprosopus, who is called אין (*Non Ens*).—*Id.
Rab.*, § 83.

It is written (*Ps.* xliv. 24), "Awake! why steepest thou,
O Lord?" And again (2 *Kings* xix. 16), "Open, Lord,
thine eyes, and see." The eye of the Macroprosopus is
always opened for good; but sometimes the eyes of the
Microprosopus are opened for evil. Woe to him upon
whom those eyes so open that they are seen mixed
with red, and with the redness glaring as an adversary
upon him who beholds it! Who shall escape from those
eyes?—*Id. Rab.*, § 153–155.

The eyes of the White Head are not like other
eyes; for they have neither eyelids nor eyebrows over
them.—*Id. Rab.*, § 112. Now, whatsoever worketh
through mercy needs neither a covering upon the eye,
nor yet eyebrows; much less does the White Head
require eyelids and eyebrows.—*Id. Rab.*, § 115. For the
White Head sleeps never, and requires no protection for
its eyes.—*Id. Rab.*, § 113. Nothing is over the eye of the
White Head to protect it; for itself protects all things,
and watches all things; and, by reason of the inspection
of this eye, all things consist. If this eye should be shut
for a single instant, nothing what ever would subsist.—
Id. Rab., § 135, 136. If the superior eye should not look
on the inferior eye, the world would cease to be.—*Id.
Rab.*, § 142.

The black color in the eyes of the Microprosopus is like that of the Stone which comes forth out of the Abyss into the great sea once in a thousand years. When that Stone appears, there are storms and tempests in the sea, and the voice of the waves is lifted up; and that voice is heard by the great fish, who is Leviathan.—*Id. Rab.*, § 632, 633.

When sins are multiplied in the world, and the Sanctuary is profaned; when the male dwells far from the female; when the robust Serpent begins to raise himself up—woe to the world that nourishes itself from the then existing justice! In those days, executioners and tormentors are given to the world, and many just men are taken out of it. Why? Because the male is separated from the female—justice from judgment."—*Id. Sut.*, § 367–369.

The ninth sephirah is called by many names; as the Covenant of the Lord, the Covenant of Circumcision, the Member of the Covenant, El Chai, the Redeeming Angel, the Fountain of the Water of Life, the Tree of Knowledge of Good and Evil, Mount Zion, Leviathan, the Lord upon the Ark of the Covenant, the Column of Peace, Time, the Gate of Tears, and the like.

THE SEPHIROTH — MATRONA

The tenth sephirah, מלכות (*Melcuth*, Royalty), is known by many names, among which the following may be mentioned: the Wife of the Microprosopus, the Earth, the Moon, the End, the Spouse, the Church of Israel, the Virgin of Israel, the House of David, the Temple of the King, the Ark of the Covenant, the Coping Stone, Shechinah, the Book of Life, and the like. The upper part of this wife of the Microprosopus is called Leah, the wife of Israel: the lower part is called Rachel, the wife of Jacob. Melcuth, or Matrona, is ACTUALITY. Things that exist in the first nine sephiroth only, are potential, invisible, and have no subsistence outside of the world of pure emanation. Things that exist in all of the ten sephiroth are actual and visible. Matrona lends visibility and actuality to that which, without her aid, would exist virtually only.

We will explain the nature of this tenth sephirah, not in our own words, which might prove inadequate, but in the words of the Idra Suta itself:

> The Microprosopus is formed in the analogy of man; and in him the disposition of the sexes, as male and female, begins at the back.—§ 945. For, in one and the same body, this man (the Microprosopus) is both male and female.— § 949. Thus the Microprosopus is a man and a woman, who adhere to each other by their backs; having four arms and four legs (two of each in front belonging to the man, and two behind belonging to the woman).—§ 997. The female head, which is at the back of the male head, is completely hidden under the hair of the Microprosopus (this hair serving as a thick veil).—§ 948.

In Plato's dialogue of the "Banquet," Socrates describes the first men as being endowed, each of them, with four arms, four legs, two faces, &c. It was a common belief, in the times of remote antiquity, that the first men were created male-female.

The masculine term of a contradiction-pregnant is impulsive and initiative: the feminine term is responsive and resistant. If these two are conjoined, back to back, so that they face away from each other, the lines of their actions will be in opposite directions, and the two terms will reciprocally annul each other. This is the equilibrium of negation and living-death. Now, since the happiness of every creature is in the exercise of its natural activities, the complete equilibrium of negation between two living creatures is nothing other than the perfected unhappiness, the entire misery, of both of them. In such equilibrium, each annuls every faculty, capacity, and activity of the other. When, however, the two terms are brought, on the contrary, face to face, each faculty or capacity of the one gives the means and the occasion for the development of a correlative faculty or capacity in the other; and then the equilibrium of synthesis takes the place of the equilibrium of reciprocal negation, and happiness takes the place of misery. Actions determined by imperfect equilibrium of negation are usually half-actions, each one contradicting its antecedent and its consequent, like the strokes of a pendulum: every one of them involves disorder and suffering. An imperfect equilibrium of synthesis is, on the contrary, a condition of progressive improvement or deterioration. Every man carries on his back the burthen of the fatality which inheres in his own nature. When he brings that burthen to the front, by obtaining a distinct understanding of it, and by deliberately accepting himself for better or worse, the fatality of his nature becomes to him a basis of actuality, on which he may build up the structure of his own destiny. Evil is incompleteness, especially incompleteness of action. None but men of integrity are happy. It is only by integrity of action that men become whole. Holiness is wholeness, integrity: willful lack of integrity is sin.

It is the doctrine of the Kabbalah, that the woman, as originally conjoined with the man, back to back, in one complex person, is necessarily evil; because misplaced, if for no other reason. When the man and the woman are separated from each other, the woman ceases to be evil. The woman becomes positively good as soon as she is brought into communication, face to face, with the man. The ldra Suta says,

> The voice of the woman (as conjoined back to back with the man), turpitude; the hair of this woman, turpitude; the legs of this woman, turpitude; the hands of this woman, turpitude; the feet of this woman, turpitude.— § 965. When the male and female elements were to be separated, an ecstatic (magnetic) trance fell upon the Microprosopus, and the female part was severed from his back, and hidden until the time when she was to be brought to the male.—§ 1028. Meanwhile malignant

> spirits, authors of disorder, were coming into being:
> but, before they were finished, Matrona came in her
> true form, and sat down before them, and the creation
> of them ceased, so that they were not finished; because
> the Matron sat down with the Holy King (the sixth
> sephirah), and associated with him face to face.—§
> 1035, 1036.

We learn from the first chapter of Genesis, that Adam was made, on the sixth day of the creation, not as a single person or as a single pair, but as a collective multitude of individuals. It is written, "In the image of God created he *him*; male and female created he *them*. And God blessed *them*, and said unto *them*," &c. The Kabbalah says that each Adamic individual was male-female, composed of a man and a woman conjoined back to back, and therefore incapable of associating with each other. It was in this fact of the non-association of the man and the woman that Adam's original "loneliness" consisted.

At the end of the sixth day, "God saw every thing he had made; and, behold, it was *very good*." But a change took place on the sabbath of rest; for, farther on, we read (ch. ii. 18), "The Lord God said, It is *not good* that Adam should be *alone*." That which is not good is evil. Evil was therefore in the world before Eve ate the apple; yea, before Eve existed as a separated person. And it was as a remedy for already existing evil that the original Adam was split lengthwise, along the part where the back now is, and made to be אִישׁ (*Ish*, man) and אִשָּׁה (*Ishah*, woman). The Idra Rabba says,

> When the Elder of elders wills to separate the male and
> female elements, he causes an ecstasy to fall upon the
> Microprosopus, and severs the woman from his back.
> He then completes all her conformations, and hides her
> until the day in which she is to be brought to the male.
> And this is what is written (*Gen.* ii, 21), "And the Lord
> God caused a deep sleep to fall upon Adam," &c.—§
> 1026–1030.

R. Simon says,

> In no day of my life have I omitted the three feasts; and,
> on account of them, I had no occasion to fast on the
> sabbath days. I had no occasion to fast on other days,
> much less on the sabbath; for whoso correctly conducts
> himself respecting those three feasts is an adept in perfect
> truth. The first feast is Matrona (the tenth sephirah); the
> second is the Holy King (the sixth sephirah); and the
> third is the Most Holy Elder, hidden in all occultations
> (the first sephirah).[24]

Matrona, as separated from the Microprosopus, is represented
in the emblematic picture by the small conical figure at the bottom,
beneath the band.

It now devolves upon us to explain the signification of the serpent which forms the framing of the picture. This serpent represents the force of fatality, and holds his tail in his mouth to denote
eternity and the eternally-recurring circulation of antecedents and
consequents. It is written in the Zeniutha:

> The vehemency (the realm of Matrona) was real, but
> within the limitations of the formlessness and emptiness
> and darkness that were on the face of the Abyss, and
> thus only. Excavation of excavations under the form
> of a serpent, far extended here and there. His tail is in
> his head. (With him, the ending is at the beginning; for
> he holds his tail in his mouth, and forms a circle.) He
> carries his head around the back (of Matrona). He is full
> of wrath, and observes. He is hidden and revealed in one
> of the thousand shorter days (in one of the numerations

---

[24] The ending of the Lord's Prayer, as it is printed in the Protestant Bibles, "For thine
is the *kingdom* (Royalty, Matrona), and the *power* (Netsech, the seventh sephirah),
and the *glory* (Hod, the eighth sephirah)," is distinctly kabbalistic, and possibly an
interpolation of some early commentator: it is neither printed in the Catholic Bibles,
nor sung in the Catholic churches.

of the Microprosopus). He was changed in his slaying, and came forth other, and castrate. As it is written (*Ps.* lxxiv. 13), "Thou breakest the heads of the dragons in the waters." Two heads there were; but one only remains.—Ch. i. § 23–31.

The Ten Sephiroth

The tabular list of the ten sephiroth, their names being given in plain English, is as follows:

(1) Thought.

(3) Understanding.   (2) Wisdom.
————————————

(5) Justice.   (4) Mercy.

(6) Beauty.
————————————

(8) Strength.   (7) Energy.

(9) Working-Power.
————————————

(10) Actuality.

Energy, Mercy, and Wisdom are the *right-hand column, the pillar of Jachin,* and the three aspects of the masculine principle.

Strength, Justice, and Understanding are *the left-hand column, the pillar of Boaz,* and the three aspects of the feminine principle.

The synthetic sephiroth, four in number, Actuality, Working-Power, Beauty, and Thought, form the famous *middle column,* which is known as a Tree of Life.

In the Greater Assembly, the companions were so seated that they became an emblematic figure of the three columns of the sephiroth. We read in the Idra Rabba,

R. Simon said to the companions, How long shall
we remain sitting here as a sole column? (or remain
unorganized.)—§ 1. Then the companions that were
before R. Simon were numbered; and there were found
present R. Eliezar, who was R. Simon's son; R. Abba;
R. Jehudah; R. Jose, son of Jacob; R. Isaac; R. Chiskia,
son of Raf; R. Chija; R. Jose; and R. Jesa. (Nine in
all, and, including R. Simon, *ten*—the number of the
sephiroth.)—§ 7. So they gave their hands to R. Simon,
and raised their fingers on high (they made the signs),
and then entered into the field, and sat down among the
trees (in the valley that stretches due E. and W. under the
canopy of heaven).—§ 8. R. Simon called R. Eliezar,
his son, and directed him to sit down before him, with
R. Abba on the opposite side. And he said, *We are
now a type of all things: this far the columns are made
firm.*—§ 13. . . . . Before the companions went out of
this field, three of them died—R. Jose, R. Chiskia, and
R. Jesa. [Ten went in, and only seven came out.]

The companions were seated in the relative positions indicated by the figure in the
margin. R. Simon sat in the first place (that
of the Crown), and the serving-brother in
the tenth place (that of Matrona, Royalty).
The beginning was in the ending: 1 was
10; for he who was master of them all was
also the servant of them all. They sat as
three triads of triads, with an appendix
(10); and the appendix was the sabbath
of rest for them all. R. Simon sat facing
the companions, and the companions sat
facing R. Simon.

```
       1.
    3.   2.
  _____
    5.   4.
       6.
  _____
    8.   7.
       9.
  _____
      10.
```

To show that the three triads were one triad, we draw a diagonal
line from 2 to 8, and that line will pass through 6: that is to say, in
order to form one triad of the three triads, we take the subjective

term of the intellectual triad, or 2, Wisdom, as male; the objective term of the physical triad, or 8, Strength, as female; and the synthetic term of the moral and synthetic triad, or 6, Beauty, as the junction of the two—and we obtain the formula,

WISDOM, STRENGTH, AND BEAUTY;

a formula not unknown to such as know the acacia.

If we bring down the first triad (1, 2, and 3) so that it shall become interlaced with the second triad, the two will form a Blazing Star, resting on its lower point, which is 6, Beauty. The first six sephiroth are the six points of the Blazing Star. On some occasions, the middle column is regarded as ending at 6, Beauty, and as bearing the Blazing Star for its ornamented capital; or, which is the same thing, as bearing the Cubical Stone. The middle column, as ending with Beauty, and as bearing the Cubical Stone, is called the Column of Beauty. It is also called the short column, because it comprises *in its shaft* the sephiroth 10, 9, and 6, and nothing higher; and the twisted column, because it is the synthesis of Jachin and Boaz, inclining first towards the one, and then towards the other, so as to be twisted as well as short. To denote its perfection and spotlessness, it is said to be made of clear white marble.

By the explanation of them in the light of the sephiroth (numerations or powers), which are intelligible principles, the תולדת (*Tholodoth*, lists of generations) mentioned in the Bereshith become available for the forecasting of the destinies of nations, churches, and other human institutions; for the *tholodoth* give, in their serial order, the successive steps of the development of principles embodied in social organizations. We will illustrate this matter by examples. If we study the existing situation of France, and remember the recent consecutive steps by which she became what she now is, we obtain several characteristic terms of a special series. We may then look into the Bereshith to find that special series. Applying the existing situation of France to the term in the series of the Bereshith to which it corresponds, we are furnished, in the next term of the series of the Bereshith, with an indication of the organic posture which France will next assume. Through this process we may obtain results characterized by a very notable degree of accuracy. The present writer has not qualified himself, by careful practice of this method, to prophesy the future of the French nation. He will state, however, for the satisfaction of the reader, that there is an extant kabbalistic prophecy, grounded on principles substantially identical with those here mentioned, that promises, for the month of November, 1879, the establishment of a universal empire, under the inspiration of France; France to be subjected, before 1879, to a process analogous with that of natural death and spiritual resurrection. This empire will be at once political and religious; will be founded on the principle of universal peace, and on a rational solution of the questions (such as those of property and labor, of women's rights, and the like) which now agitate society. It will hold the "keys of the East," and will last 354 years and 4 months without material alteration. We give this prophecy for what it is worth. We disapprove generally, and on principle, all prophecies that specify "times and hours."

The names mentioned by the Bereshith in the several lists of the generations are not at all names of men, but are names of phases of organic development. All these names are significant in Hebrew. For example, the name *Cain* signifies possession, property.[25] The name *Abel* signifies vacuity, emptiness, and, in contradistinction from that of Cain, non-possession, *pauperism*.[26] The murder of Abel by Cain is the subordination of capital by labor, and the consequent destruction of capital; for in the peculiar phase of primitive socialism denoted by the family of Cain, and whose beginning, course, and ending were known by authentic tradition to the writers of the Bereshith, it was the laborer who was the proprietor, and it was the capitalist who lived on the crumbs that fell from the laborer's table. Cain, the proprietor, was him-

---

[25] And Adam knew Eve his wife; and she conceived, and bare קִין (*Kin*, or Cain, *acquisition*); and she said, קָנִיתִי (*Ken*-ithi, I have *acquired*) a man with Jehovah. —Gen. iv. 1.

[26] הֶבֶל He-bel, *empty breath, vanity.*

self a tiller of the soil, and his children were the inventors of the mechanic arts. Abel, on the other hand, was a priest; and the priesthood, in the early days, comprised all professional men who did not work with their hands, and all general directors of industry. When Cain slew Abel, he rendered the social synthesis impossible: he destroyed that which had been created to make him, Cain, rich. *Seth* signifies stability, basis, and, in the social sphere, order.[27] Seth is despotism—is the political and social structure that was built up, as it respects its chief corner-stone, upon the dead body of the pauper Abel.[28]

Adam was never "perfect in his generations": he never walked truly with the Elohim. At first, Cain and Abel were in the earth, without Seth; and, afterwards, Cain and Seth were in it, without Abel. Always one whole side of the mystical triangle was lacking. It became necessary, therefore, in the plan of Divine Providence, that the primitive humanity should be drowned out.

Noah was "a just man, and *perfect in his generations;* and Noah walked with the Elohim. And Noah begat three sons, Shem, Ham, and Japhet." Ham is the new Cain, and Japhet is the new Abel.

The times have changed. To-day it is Abel that slays Cain, capital that robs labor. Seth reigns to-day, as he did before the flood; but he founds his sovereignty to-day, not upon the tyranny of labor, but upon the tyranny of capital.

The list of the generations from Adam to Lamech—Adam, Cain, Enoch, Irad, Mehujael, Methusael, Lamech—gives a perfect series of seven terms. Lamech lived 777 years. "All the days of Lamech were seven hundred seventy and seven years; and he died." The generations from Seth to Noah, including Seth and Noah, give a perfect series of nine terms, or a triad of triads.

The numbers three, seven, and nine, are holy numbers.

The generations of Japhet, from Gomer to Tiras, form a regular

---

[27] And Adam knew his wife again; and he bare a son, and called his name שת (*Sheth, appointed, founded*); because God has appointed to me, she said (שתלי *Sheth-*li), another seed instead of Abel, whom Cain slew.—*Gen.* iv 25.

[28] *Seth* and *Satan* are different forms of the same word.

series of seven terms. The generations of Ham, from Cush (Asiatic Ethiopia) to Nimrod (Babylon), give a series of seven terms. The generations of Ham, through Misraim (Egypt) to Philistim, give a triad of triads.

Matthew says (chap. i. ver. 17), "All the generations from Abraham to David are fourteen (2 x 7) generations; and from David unto the carrying-away into Babylon are fourteen (2 x 7) generations; and from the carrying-away into Babylon unto Christ are fourteen (2 x 7) generations." There were in all, therefore, from Abraham to Christ, forty-two (6 x 7) generations. This summing-up agrees neither with Matthew's own list of names, nor with the Old-Testament record; but it shows the influence, upon the evangelist's mind, of the Old-Testament philosophy of numbers. If we take the list given by Luke, and count from Christ, through Joseph, to Isaac, we find fifty-four (6 x 9) generations. Adding to these six series of nines the series of nines from Abraham, through Arphaxad, to Shem, and the series of nines from Noah, through Seth, to Adam, we have just eight series of nines. According to Luke, therefore, Jesus was born at the end of the eighth epoch of nines, in a grand logical series of nines, or triad of triads, commencing at the foundation of human society. According to Matthew, he was born at the end of the sixth series of sevens, in a grand logical series of sevens, commencing with Abraham.

We had occasion to mention, a moment ago, but without indorsing them, certain prophetic intimations respecting the destinies of France, and the establishment, in the year 1879, of a universal empire. We have no exact knowledge of the process, in its details, by which the special results were obtained, but are informed that the prophecy is grounded, generally, on the interpretation of a Sabæan series of 7's, not given in the Bereshith, or given in it, if at all, under some disguised form. The series is as follows: 1. Saturn; 2. Venus; 3. Jupiter; 4. Mercury; 5. Mars; 6. Luna; 7. Sol: which is the series, but read backward, of the planets that govern the characteristics, and the order of succession, of the seven days of the week; for Saturday is Saturn's day, Friday is Venus's (or Friga's) day, Thursday is Jupiter's (or Thor's) day; and so on.

The prophecy in question turns, like other prophecies of similar nature, on the observed fact, that history continually repeats itself; going through one completed revolution of events after another, each revolution being the reproduction, not by the way of identity, but by *the way of analogy*, of the revolutions that preceded it. Human evolutions take effect in upward spiral movements, and in ever-recurring circles that rise continually one above another, as circles succeed each other in the winding stairways on the outside of the terraced, mound-shaped temples of remote antiquity.

It is the serpent—the order of fatality which is without admixture of liberty—not human history, that gnaws its own tail, and reproduces itself in ever-recurring identical circles. Human history repeats itself, but always on higher and higher planes.

The true religion that exists now, always has existed, and always will exist, among men: but it has presented itself, in ever-recurring circles, under higher and higher forms; and men have interpreted it differently, according to their varying intellectual and moral capacities, and according to the progressive spirit of the different ages. Christ is the Lamb that was slain from the foundation of the world. No true religious institution is ever abolished by the new institution that replaces it; for the new institution is the old institution itself, but transfigured and glorified. Christianity is the rejuvenation and glorification of the Hebrew religion; just as the Hebrew religion was the transfiguration and rejuvenation of the Hamitic religions which preceded it, and had their seats in Egypt and Babylon. Christianity came to fulfill the law and the prophets; not to destroy them. An approaching rejuvenation of the Christian religion is clearly foretold in the New Testament. The second coming of Jesus, and his reign of a thousand years upon the earth, are written beforehand with letters of light in the books of the Christian dispensation. The prophecies of the Old Testament, foretelling the end of the Jewish Church and the establishment of a new one, are darkness itself when compared with the promises of glory contained in the Apocalypse of St. John.

If the above-sketched theory be valid, the destinies of the Christian Church will be a transformed analogical reproduction, point for point, of the destinies of the Hebrew Church; just as the destinies of the Hebrew (or Shemitic) Church were an analogical reproduction, point for point, of the destinies of the Hamitic Church which preceded it. Tracing the analogies, comparing them, and verifying the accuracy of their sequence in the order of the series, we find ourselves—or, at the least, we appear to find ourselves: who knows?—to be living in a period analogically resembling the times just preceding the Jewish captivity. We are to look, therefore, for the appearance, in the immediate future, of a transfigured Nebuchadnezzar at the head of a transfigured Chaldean empire, and for an approaching captivity of the Church in some transfigured Babylon; the Church to be delivered in due time from captivity, and restored to its former seat (but shorn of its initiative) by some transfigured Cyrus at the head of an army of transfigured Medes and Persians.

This same series of the seven planets, read, not backward, but forward, in the direct order of the days of the week, is evil and disastrous; for its progress is not then upward and onward, but distinctly downward. In it every planet (except Sol, who stands always in the seventh place, or in the house of redemption) is afflicted, and sheds deleterious influence.

This series of evil begins with Luna, whose portrait is given in the margin.[29]

---

[29] The pictures here reproduced may be found in the books of Eliphaz Levi. They were communicated to the writer, with several others of like character, by that enthusiastic student of kabbalistic Masonry, the Hon. Charles Levi Woodbury. The Latin of the inscriptions, and especially the bad Latin of some of them, and several other indications, lead us to believe that the pictures have come down to us with many supposed improvements. The writer is alone responsible for the explanations given in the text: no such explanations came with the pictures as he received them.

The picture represents the boat of the moon, with the "Torch-bearer" sailing in it, under the rays of the detestable inverted five-pointed star. The star is not before the figure, to serve, detestable though it be, as an ideal of life and conduct, but is vertically above it, as an unseen compressive power. The wings denote initiative faculty. The "Torch-bearer" is a law to himself: he follows no ideal, but carries his own incendiary light. Obstinate, suspicious, and self-sufficient, he dreads nothing so much as the possibility that he may convict himself, before witnesses, of lack of almighty power. Utterly selfish, and acting always on the maxim, "Self-preservation is the first law of nature," he passes like water, and without noticing the transitions, from one iniquity to another, and wanes and waxes and changes as the moon waxes and changes; for it is under the moon's malign aspect that this lunatic lives and moves. He is ignorant of himself, but knows darkly the things that are not himself, and calumniates them. In all things he is perverse.

When many "Torch-bearers" are placed in the same field of action, they form self-interested cliques and rings that come into antagonism with each other. All of them acknowledging that "might makes right," supremacy naturally gravitates into the hands of violent desperadoes, and the weaker parties become fags and slaves of the stronger. The portrait of "Nembroud," the typical desperado, will be found on the opposite page.[30] He bears the crown, to denote his authority; and the sword, to denote the source of his authority. This typical king of spades bears also a shield, with a device on it, which is the Tower of Babel; and this device denotes the ultimate futility of all his undertakings.

The fags and slaves of Nembroud learn, in the experience of their abject condition, the vices that are appropriate to fags and slaves. They become reticent, forecasting, treacherous, and cunning; and the distinct consciousness of their own inherent villainy forces itself upon them. Through the fact of this consciousness the star of their

---

[30] France was in the hands of lunatics when Nembroud-Bonaparte throttled her: we speak here of the great Napoleon, not the little one. The lesser Bonaparte was not Nembroud, but Acham, whose portrait will be given a little farther on.

villainy passes from its occult position overhead, and places itself in front as an accepted ideal of life and conduct. They were knaves before they were fags and slaves; but, as expert fags and slaves, they become conscious and politic knaves.

The portrait of "Tharthac," the typical politic knave, is given below, in the margin.

When Baron Nembroud establishes his power with a high hand, the serf Tharthac escapes to some free city, sets up a banking-house, and ruins Nembroud by lending him money at usurious rates of interest on securities deposited in the free city. For Nembroud cannot carry on his pillaging expeditions without that very assistance of Tharthac which ruins him, Nembroud: therefore Nembroud detests Tharthac. Genuine nobles and aristocrats always hate successful business-men who deal in money. But Tharthac, no matter how rich he may become, or what high titles he may achieve, can never be a real aristocrat, or substitute himself in the place of Nembroud; for genuine nobility always originates in highway robbery, armed pillage, and the power of the sword—never in usurious gains, fraudulent commerce, shoddy-contracts, perversion of public funds, and the power of the strong-box.[31]

---

[31] It was under the Orleans dynasty, which is his authentic embodiment, that Tharthac shone, with transcendent splendor, in the realm of France.

When his Majesty the Emperor Nembroud is engaged in foreign wars, Tharthac-Talleyrand, Tharthac-Fouché, and their like, work themselves into his confidence, and become his trusted ministers.

Nembroud never fails to be betrayed at the critical moment. This fact is placed beyond doubt by the almost unvarying testimony of history. The knaves held in subjection by Nembroud, and the knaves who have acted as his instruments, join hands with the knaves and desperadoes who are his avowed and official enemies. Nembroud's armies become demoralized by the defection, and are defeated at the end in every encounter, as Napoleon I and Sardanapalus, and their like, stand ready to testify. New rulers are raised up; and a new order of things is inaugurated—one not based precisely on violence, or precisely on fraud, but rather on a happy synthetic combination of violence with fraud.

The portrait of "Acham," the representative of legalized scoundrelism, and the legitimate defender of frauds (interests) organized into institutions, is given on the opposite page. Acham seems, from his attitude in the picture, to be all right; and he would be all right, were it not for the presence of the little devil that holds up his train.[32]

"Nahema" (sometimes wrongly taken for "Lilith," who is Satan's wife)[33] is the representative of the special wide-spread, all-pervading, and inevitable corruption that eats out the heart of iniquitous and falsely-refined societies. She seduces Acham, leads him astray, and causes him to destroy himself by his own folly. She reigned triumphantly in the times of the regency in France, was the principal ornament of the court circles of Napoleon III, and graced

---

[32] Napoleon III was Nembroud-Acham: M. Thiers is Tharthac-Acham.

[33] According to the Kabbala, there art three chief devils: the first is named *Thohu*; the second, *Bohu*; and the third, *Thehom*. The seven tabernacles, or hells, are seven deadly vices. Samaël, the Angel of Death, rules over the whole. Samaël, evil desire, Satan, and the serpent that seduced Eve, are the same thing. Samaël's wife is called the Strumpet: he and she, united, are called the Beast. This Strumpet is the Talmudic *Lilith*.

the banqueting-table of Belshazzar when he was slain in his own palace by the Medes and Persians. Her mighty deeds are everywhere spoken of in history. Her portrait will be found in the margin.

"Nabam," the personage whose portrait is given on the next page, is the gentleman in the clerk's office, with whom we, all of us, whether collective peoples or individual men and women, will have to settle our accounts, Saturday night, for the week's work. Nabam is Saturn, Nahema is Venus, Acham is Jupiter, Tharthac is Mercury, Nembroud is Mars, and the Light-bearer is the Moon; and all of them, as here depicted, are shining with malignant aspect. And thus ends the eventful history of the life and adventures of "Mr. Badman."

The characteristics of the planets, as afflicted, are here given in some detail, and their normal characteristics are analogous to those stated, but opposite. If the reader desires a more full account of the characteristics of the several planets, he may find it in any good book of astrology.

CONCLUSION

Thus far we have been able, and with no little difficulty, to trace, in a very superficial manner, the deep doctrine

of the Kabbalah. Our exposition is wholly inadequate, and perhaps, in some minor points, incorrect; for the texts we have interpreted are very dark. We trust, however, that what we have said will suffice to break the ten seals of the lesser Zohar, and to make it an open book.